Contents

Introduction

Globalisation – Good or Bad? is Volume 305 in the **ISSUES** series. The aim of the series is to offer current, diverse information about important issues in our world, from a UK perspective.

ABOUT GLOBALISATION – GOOD OR BAD?

Today's world is becoming ever more connected. It has never been easier to do business with other countries. Globalisation is in its prime – or is it? This book explores the topic of globalisation from many different perspectives. Some think it is in decline, others think it will continue to grow, or change shape. It also looks at technicalities such as sanctions, trade deals and fair trade, as well as exploring the very early days of the Brexit effect.

OUR SOURCES

Titles in the **ISSUES** series are designed to function as educational resource books, providing a balanced overview of a specific subject.

The information in our books is comprised of facts, articles and opinions from many different sources, including:

⇨ Newspaper reports and opinion pieces

⇨ Website factsheets

⇨ Magazine and journal articles

⇨ Statistics and surveys

⇨ Government reports

⇨ Literature from special interest groups.

A NOTE ON CRITICAL EVALUATION

Because the information reprinted here is from a number of different sources, readers should bear in mind the origin of the text and whether the source is likely to have a particular bias when presenting information (or when conducting their research). It is hoped that, as you read about the many aspects of the issues explored in this book, you will critically evaluate the information presented.

It is important that you decide whether you are being presented with facts or opinions. Does the writer give a biased or unbiased report? If an opinion is being expressed, do you agree with the writer? Is there potential bias to the 'facts' or statistics behind an article?

ASSIGNMENTS

In the back of this book, you will find a selection of assignments designed to help you engage with the articles you have been reading and to explore your own opinions. Some tasks will take longer than others and there is a mixture of design, writing and research-based activities that you can complete alone or in a group.

FURTHER RESEARCH

At the end of each article we have listed its source and a website that you can visit if you would like to conduct your own research. Please remember to critically evaluate any sources that you consult and consider whether the information you are viewing is accurate and unbiased.

Useful weblinks

www.theconversation.com

www.coolgeography.co.uk

www.economicshelp.org

www.fairtrade.org.uk

www.fairtradefederation.org

globalconnections.hsbc.com

globalisationtimelineproject.wordpress.com

GOV.UK

www.theguardian.com

blogs.lse.ac.uk

www.mckinsey.com

www.mintel.com

parliament.uk

www.pressassociation.com

www.telegraph.co.uk

www.wto.org

www.youtube.com/user/explainitychannel

Globalisation – Good or Bad?

Independence Educational Publishers

First published by Independence Educational Publishers

The Studio, High Green

Great Shelford

Cambridge CB22 5EG

England

© Independence 2016

ISBN-13: 978 1 86168 750 0

Printed in Great Britain

Zenith Print Group

What is globalisation?

Globalisation is a widely discussed topic; it is therefore not all that easy to explain in simple words.

Let's start from the beginning with a background to globalisation.

Advances in technology such as mobile phones, aeroplanes, and the Internet have made the growth of transport and communication networks possible. Amongst other things, this means that people and countries can exchange information and goods more quickly, and in a less complicated way. This process is called 'globalisation'.

Globalisation comes from 'globe' and means the worldwide coming together of countries and nations. Let's look at an example.

Companies used to manufacture products in their home countries, just like the (imaginary) companies 'Profi-TV' and 'SuperColor', who produce televisions in Country A. Their products are in direct competition with one another but both companies pay the same salaries and production costs, they have the same customers, use similar suppliers, and both sell televisions at similar prices. In short, the same conditions apply to both companies. So far, so good. Due to technical, cultural and economic developments that have come about through globalisation, however, other companies, which manufacture products under different conditions, can now offer their products in Country A too. So, a company from Country B can sell televisions in Country A at a lower price, because they were produced for less. The local firms Profi-TV and SuperColor have to react to withstand the competition.

And so, the world grows closer together and there is an active exchange of goods between countries. More affordable products are available for more people. However, not only does an exchange of products and economic goods take place, but also of services, knowledge, cultural goods and even languages. All of these individual elements are closely linked and influence each other.

But where there is light, there is also shadow.

Because of globalisation and this intense exchange of goods, people and the environment often suffer. If a company decides to move production to an economically disadvantaged country, people in

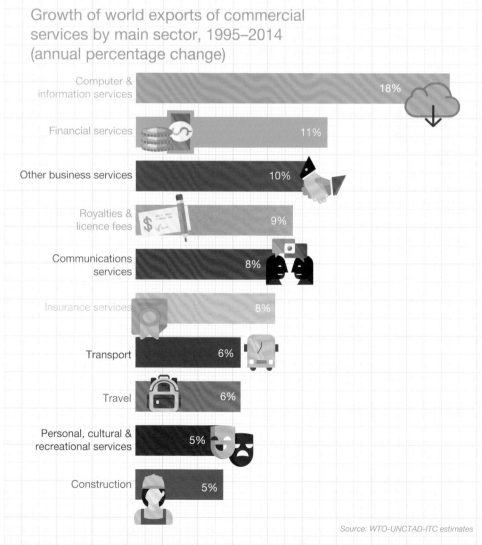

Growth of world exports of commercial services by main sector, 1995–2014 (annual percentage change)

Sector	%
Computer & information services	18%
Financial services	11%
Other business services	10%
Royalties & licence fees	9%
Communications services	8%
Insurance services	8%
Transport	6%
Travel	6%
Personal, cultural & recreational services	5%
Construction	5%

Source: WTO-UNCTAD-ITC estimates

industrialised countries lose their jobs. At the same time, job opportunities open up to many locals in the economically disadvantaged country. Many people in these countries work for very little money in comparison to those in industrialised countries. Therefore, they often remain poor and more often than not, do not have sufficient social insurance or health insurance cover.

A further disadvantage of globalisation is ecological problems such as climate change. The use of aeroplanes, ships and lorries to transport goods over international borders is constantly on the increase, this causes more carbon dioxide to be released into the atmosphere which, in turn, is the main cause of global warming.

Even national environmental standards are ignored, this is a further cost factor in the worldwide site competition which should be kept as low as possible in order to be attractive for a company.

There are, therefore, many sides to globalisation which affect all aspects of life. What's important is to realise that globalisation itself is neither good or bad, it just depends how people deal with all the new possibilities in the future.

11 July 2013

⇨ The above information is the transcript of a YouTube video by explainity and it is printed here with kind permission. Please visit https://www.youtube.com/user/explainitychannel to view this video, and others.

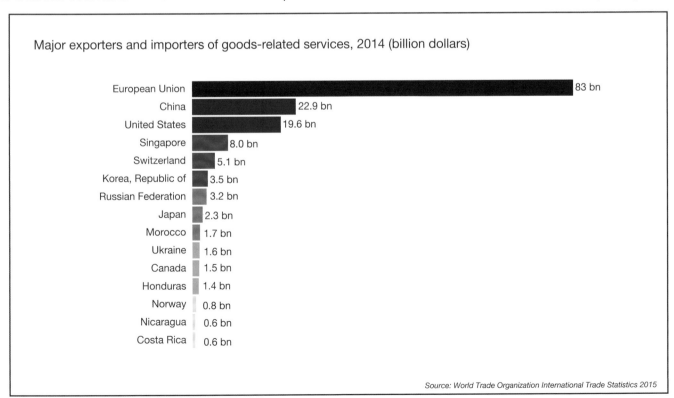

Major exporters and importers of goods-related services, 2014 (billion dollars)

European Union	83 bn
China	22.9 bn
United States	19.6 bn
Singapore	8.0 bn
Switzerland	5.1 bn
Korea, Republic of	3.5 bn
Russian Federation	3.2 bn
Japan	2.3 bn
Morocco	1.7 bn
Ukraine	1.6 bn
Canada	1.5 bn
Honduras	1.4 bn
Norway	0.8 bn
Nicaragua	0.6 bn
Costa Rica	0.6 bn

Source: World Trade Organization International Trade Statistics 2015

Globalisation – a timeline

Year	Popular, cultural and scientific reference	Economic reference	Political and social reference
Late prehistoric period 1000–3500 BCE	Migration from Africa continues throughout prehistory. ca 9500 BCE onwards – food surpluses lead to population increase and construction of permanent villages.	End of the epoch sees growing modes of exchange between a growing number of people in many regions of the world.	Social structure begins to appear as chiefs and priests are exempt from hard manual labour. Farming societies support two other social classes, Crafts and Solders/Bureaucrats.
The pre-modern period 3500 BC –1500 CE	ca 3500 BCE – writing invented in Mesopotamia, Egypt and China. ca 3500 BCE – invention of the wheel. 753 BCE – Rome founded by twin brothers Romulus and Remus. 859 CE – the University of Al Karaouine in Fez, Morocco, the oldest continuously operating academic degree-granting university in the world, is founded. Chinese invention of hydraulic engineering, gun powder, mechanical clocks, paper printing. Local religions merge into the major world religions - Judaism, Christianity, Islam, Hinduism and Buddhism.	Silk Road links Chinese and Roman empires. Several interlocking trade routes are developed towards the end of the pre-modern period connecting the most populous regions of Eurasia and North Eastern Africa. The South American Aztecs develop trade links in their hemisphere.	221 BCE onwards – the Qin Emperors' armies ruled large portions of China supported by large bureaucracies. Due to new trade networks, migration increases leading to a population increase and the development of urban centres. The spread of diseases and plagues such as the Bubonic Plague (1347–1350) affects concentrated populations across the world.
The early modern period 1500–1750 CE	Atlantic slave trade results in the death and suffering of millions of non-Europeans forcing population transfers within the Americas. 1450 – Johannes Gutenberg develops the printing press. It plays a key role in the establishment of a community of scientists who can now communicate their discoveries helping to bring on the scientific revolution. 1492 – discovery of America by Christopher Columbus.	1648 – Protestant Reformation of the Catholic church fuels ideas of liberalism, intensifying the cultural and economic flows between Europe, Africa and the Americas. National joint stock companies such as the Dutch and English East India Companies set up to trade on a global level.	European metropolitan centres and merchant classes begin to appear. Monarchs of Spain, Portugal, The Netherlands, France and England allocate resources for New World exploration.
The modern period 1750–1900 CE	Newspapers begin circulation in developed countries. The invention of the telegraph (1866) and telephone (1876). 1859 – Charles Darwin publishes On the Origin of the Species. 1880s – motion picture camera invented. 1896 – first modern Olympic Games.	Australia and the Pacific Islands are incorporated into the European dominated cultural and economic exchange. 1850–1914 volume of world trade increases dramatically. Sterling-based Gold Standard introduced allowing currency to flow freely between trading countries. Railways and steam trains aid infrastructure links.	1848 – Karl Marx publishes the Communist Manifesto in London. An analytical approach to class struggle. 1863 – Discovery of germ theory leads to improvements in global public health. 1863 – Red Cross founded to provide international relief for war and disaster victims.
1900s	1903 – the Wright Brothers invent the aeroplane. 1905 – Industrial Workers of the World (IWW) founded. Einstein develops his theory of relativity.	1897 – Japan joins the Gold Standard.	1901 – first Nobel Prize awarded.
1910s	1917 – first passenger flight.		1914–18 – assassination of Archduke Franz Ferdinand leads to World War I. 1919 – Treaty of Versailles signed on 28 June by Germany and the Allied Powers. League of Nations formed as a result of the Treaty of Versailles, establishing a global political system.
1920s	1927 – development of television, transmission of first electronic TV picture. 1928 – Alexander Fleming discovers penicillin.	1929 – Wall Street Crash leads to the Great Depression, halting globalisation.	1917–21 – Russian Revolution 1921 – Communist Party founded in China. 1927 – creation of Saudi Arabia.
1930s	1930 – global radio broadcast, first broadcast relayed to 242 stations across six continents. 1937 – Hindenburg Zeppelin disaster.	Export-Import Bank of the United States finances and insures foreign purchases of American goods.	1935 – the National Labor Relations Act passes as law in the US. 1936–39 – Spanish Civil War.
1940s	1945 – America uses the atom bomb against Japan in the final stages of WWII. 1947 – invention of rocket propulsion allows space travel and introduction of satellites.	1944 – Bretton Woods economic conference establishes an international economic order.	1939-45 – World War II starts when Germany invades Poland without warning. 1945 – beginning of Cold War era. 1945 – United Nations (UN) founded. 1947 - General Agreement of Tariffs and Trade (GATT) formed. 1948 – 'Universal Declaration of Human Rights' drafted and adopted by UN. 1949 – Chinese Revolution. 1949 – NATO formed.
1950s	1955 – first McDonalds restaurant opens. 1956–1990 – African countries gain independence. 1957 - first satellite in space, Sputnuk 1. 1958 – integrated bircuit invented (computer chip) by Jack Kilby and Robert Noyce. 1959 – DNA code cracked by Watson and Crick.		1950–53 – Korean War. 1958 – European common market created to bring about economic integration between certain EU countries.
1960s	1962 – Andy Warhol painted Campbell's Soup Cans. Thought to be inspired by mass production and consumerism in the US. 1967 – 'Global Village' coined as a term. 1969 – Apollo 11, first man on the moon.	1960 – Organization of the Petroleum Exporting Countries (OPEC) formed.	1963 – Martin Luther King's "I have a dream" speech advocates global racial equality. 1965–73 – Vietnam War and subsequent anti-Vietnam protests. 1966 – International Covenant on Civil and Political Rights (ICCPR) treaty adopted by UN.

1970s	1970 – first Earth Day and founding of Greenpeace the following year. 1973 – first oil crisis. Integrated Circuit mass produced. Advances in computers, fibre optics, satellites and miniature electronics.	Global assembly lines dominate the production of manufactured goods, aided by communications developments. Developing countries spread/borrow unwisely from developed countries.	1970s – The New International Economic Order (NIEO) put forward by UN.
1980s	1980 – the first mobile phone appears. 1980 – first cases of HIV/AIDS identified in the US. 1985 – Chernobyl nuclear power accident.	'Third world debt' crisis begins around the globe as nations are unable to pay back debts incurred during the 1970s. 1989 – fall of the Berlin Wall signals the end of the Cold War leaving Capitalism as the only dominant economic system in the world.	
1990s	1991 – environmental justice movement. 1991 – World Wide Web invented by Tim Berners-Lee enabling further instant communications around the world. 1996 – Dolly the sheep. The world's first cloned mammal.	Regional and bilateral Trade Agreements multiply around the world. 1997 – Asian financial crisis. US Trans-national companies (TNC's) such as Enron engage in fraud and subsequently collapse.	1991 – Gulf War. 1995 – World Trade Organization (WTO) founded, replacing GATT. 1999 – anti-globalisation protest in Seattle surrounding the WTO conference.
2000s	2001 – World Trade Center, New York, US, attacked by terrorists. 2004 – Space Ship One, the first privately funded space mission. 2003 – social networking site Facebook invented by Mark Zuckerberg, providing a platform for millions of people to interact daily worldwide.	2007 – US sub-prime lending collapse leads to a systemic global financial crisis. 2001 – US stock market plummets after 9/11. 2000 – wealthy countries agree to partial third world debt cancellation. 2002 – Euro begins circulation and is adopted as official currency by 16 of the 27 members of the EU. 2000 – Non-Governmental Organizations (NGOs) call for the cancellation of third world debt on the 50th anniversary of the World Bank and IMF. 2009 – collapse of Lehman Brothers leads to global financial and economic meltdown.	2000 – World leaders gather for UN Millennium Summit, agreeing to the eradication of world poverty by 2015. War in Afghanistan. US declares 'War on Terror'. 2003 – Iraq War and subsequent global anti-war protests. 2009 – UN Climate Change Conference in Copenhagen.

Effects of globalisation on the UK economy

Globalisation involves the increased integration and interdependence of the global economy. It means there will be a rise in trade, and increase in movement of labour and capital.

Some of the effects of globalisation on the UK economy

⇨ Comparative advantage. UK firms can benefit from specialising in goods where they have a comparative advantage. This will also lead to lower prices for consumers.

⇨ Shifting sectors: Globalisation will lead to a shift in the sectors of the economy. For example, the UK no longer has a comparative advantage in many manufacturing industries. Developing countries now have an advantage due to lower labour costs. This process can lead to temporary structural unemployment. But these effects can be offset by specialisation in other areas, e.g. in Financial and insurance services.

⇨ Increased competition. Globalisation means that domestic monopolies will now face more international competition. This will help reduce costs and prices for firms.

⇨ Migration. Globalisation makes it easier for migrants to enter and work in the UK. This can help the UK fill job vacancies. However, it can also place greater stress on UK housing and public services because of the net migration of people into the UK.

⇨ Global economic cycle. The UK is more affected by the global economic cycle. For example, a deep recession in the EU will affect the UK, because we rely on the EU to export many goods. The global credit crunch had a very damaging impact on the UK economy because we are affected by financial crises in other countries.

Globalisation – factors and dimensions

Globalisation refers to the process by which the world's local and regional economies, societies and cultures have become integrated together through a global network of communication, transportation and trade. With reference to industry it is also the shift to a globalised economic system dominated by supranational (across and above the governments of nations) corporate trade and banking institutions.

There are three main forms of globalisation:

1. Economic globalisation – the growth and spread of transnational corporations, the rise of NICs, the rise of global economic institutions like the IMF and World Bank.

2. Cultural globalisation – initially this was the impact of Western culture, art, media, sport and leisure pursuits on the rest of the world. This is now a multidirectional process, as cultural aspects move all over the globe through the Internet and migration. Hollywood is now rivalled by Bollywood and Nollywood for example!

3. Political globalisation – institutions like the United Nations, regional trading blocs and particularly the influence of western democracies and their affect on poor countries have resulted in political globalisation.

The history of globalisation

Globalisation is thought of as a recent phenomenon that is driven by inventions like the airplane or the Internet. However, globalisation has been taking place for centuries; it is just that the pace of this process is accelerating.

The Silk Road is a great example of early globalisation, which spanned from Europe all the way to East Asia, moving silk and other products from as early as the 2nd century BC.

The invention of steamships and railroads expanded the process of globalisation, and humans have engaged in cultural exchange and international trade for centuries.

Some of the forerunners in globalisation were the British and Dutch, when the Dutch East India Company and the British East India Company started trading with India and then China. These trade relations have slowly been translated into globalisation or free trade. It could also be argued that the slave trade or triangular trade was another driver of globalisation.

There are different theories and ideas about globalisation, and it has its supporters and critics. Some suggest that globalisation leads to efficient use of resources and benefits all who are involved. Others dislike globalisation and claim it is increasing inequality between the very rich and the very poor.

Some major patterns of globalisation and trade are that:

MEDCs (More Economically Developed Country), or richer countries, tend to produce manufactured secondary goods such as cars or computers and sell lots of services. These are high value goods.

MEDCs also produce a lot of research and development products and services such as legal and banking services – again high value.

LDCs or the poorest countries tend to produce lower value raw materials or farm goods such as bauxite or cotton. These are primary products.

MEDCs import a lot of raw materials at low prices, but sell higher value processed goods. The MEDCs 'Win' in this process.

MEDCs make rules that limit poorer countries, ability to compete – by paying their farmers subsidies to make their goods cheaper OR taxing Imports (an import tariff). This makes trade unfair.

LEDCs often have a lot of debt so it is hard for them to start up secondary industries.

The control of the trade rests with the richer countries (MEDCs) who have the major markets and buying POWER; prices controlled on world markets so are out of poorer country control.

NICs are changing this pattern, rivalling the richer 'Western' nations – manufacturing is in decline in many MEDCs.

Trading blocs have led to trade creation between members; countries outside the bloc have suffered from trade diversion.

How is globalisation measured?

The KOF index measures social, economic and political measures of globalisation, on a scale of 0 to 100 with 100 being most globalised.

The impacts of globalisation

"We believe that the central challenge we face today is to ensure that globalisation becomes a positive force for all of the world's people."

(UN Millennium Declaration, 2000).

The table on the next page shows many of the pros and cons of globalisation, you do not need all of these, but you should know some backed up with evidence.

	Benefits	Problems
Economic	Globalisation is tied up with free trade, and this reduces the barriers that once stood between nations trading freely with one another. This means companies can profit. Examples of free trade agreements are the North American Free Trade Agreement (NAFTA), which allows Mexico, Canada and the United States to exchange products and services without significant import and export restrictions. Under both GATT and WTO, world trade has expanded rapidly.	Globalisation can lead to the 'labour drain'. Since globalisation allows workers to easily move from one country to another. This can also lead to a 'brain drain', where after receiving training in their home countries, many SKILLED people emigrate and spend their professional career in a WEALTHY economy at the expense of their home country. This costs the African continent over $4.1 billion in the employment of 150,000 expatriate professionals annually.
	Globalisation creates a steady cash flow into the poorer and indebted countries, which gradually decreases inequalities.	Some economists believe that free trade is only possible if industries in poorer countries are allowed to grow under a certain level of economic protection. This is known as the 'paradox of free trade'.
	Companies can also hire workers in foreign countries to work for them using online tools and telecommunications. This reduces company's costs. TNCs have profited from this.	Some countries can lose out on tax revenue. Since many companies are able to trade with one country while being based in another, large corporations often exploit tax havens such as Luxembourg, Switzerland and Hong Kong to avoid paying taxes in the countries where they generate their profits.
	There is a worldwide market for the companies and for the customers there is a better access to products from different countries	Globalisation has had a cultural impact on many countries that have been subject to large-scale immigration. Many critics of globalisation feel that the free movement of labour has resulted in the weakening of specific cultures.
	In many cases, free movement of labour allows economies to fix 'gaps' that exist in their labour markets. For example, the United Kingdom has hired nurses from India to fill positions in its public hospitals that were previously empty due to local labour shortages.	Specialisation of countries in one or two single products makes them particularly vulnerable to changes in the market price. If the price falls the country loses its source of income.
	Free trade also allows nations and economies to specialise, producing higher quality goods at better prices. If a country, for example, has large oil reserves but little land that's suitable for farming, it can focus on oil production while importing fresh food from abroad.	Globalisation can swamp weak economies with products, ruining local markets. In Kampala in Uganda the dumping of cheap clothes donated to charity decimated the textile industry.
Culture	Culturally we have become more open and tolerant towards each other, cultural intermingling is common and those who live in the other parts of the world appear more approachable than before.	Language differences are being eroded by the dominant language of business, English. This is putting some languages under threat of extinction.
	There is a lot of technological development that countries have undergone over the years. Thus, helping in sharing of information and technology. This helps most of the poorer nation's progress at the same speed as the rich industrialised nations.	Globalisation may lead to loss of cultural identity as Western ideas are sometimes imposed upon other nations.
	In a globalised world, workers can more easily move from one country to another to market their skills to employers and contribute to the economy.	There are some experts who think that globalisation is also leading to communicable diseases spreading (e.g. Ebola) and social degeneration.
	Consumers enjoy a greater choice of goods and services from free trade, since foreign companies can easily offer their products for sale. They also benefit from lower overall prices for goods, as a greater variety of goods for sale increases competition and drives prices down.	Corporations could end up 'ruling the world' ahead of governments because there is a lot of power and money invested by them due to globalisation. This poses problems as people in poorer countries are often exploited in 'sweatshops'.
		There is immense pressure on the employed people of rich industrialised countries who are always under the threat of their jobs being outsourced to poorer nations.
Politics	Globalisation forces politics to merge and decisions that are being taken can be beneficial to people all over the world.	Many nation states feel that they are losing control over key decisions and sacrificing their sovereignty. It is this reason that is given for the UK not joining the Euro single currency.
	Global networks give oppressed people a voice, social media was used in the Arab Spring protests for example.	The major agents of globalisation, such as the IMF and World Bank, are based in wealthier nations.
Environment	Since we share financial interests, corporations and governments are trying to sort out environmental problems for each other. The Montreal Protocol of 1987 on ozone depletion is a great example of this.	Many economists and environmentalists have criticised globalisation due to its environmental impact. This can be seen in the increasing numbers of air miles for our food and declining air quality in places like China where many manufactured goods are produced.

The above information is reprinted with kind permission from Cool Geography.
Please visit www.coolgeography.co.uk for further information.

© Cool Geography 2016

Green light for globalisation: over half of Brits have felt three or more benefits of internationalism

International influences on Britain are constantly evolving and it seems that the vast majority of consumers are benefiting as a result. New research from Mintel's flagship *British Lifestyles* report finds that three quarters (74%) of UK consumers claim to have felt at least one benefit of globalisation personally, with over half (53%) feeling three or more benefits.

What's more, the research finds that the positive influence of internationalism is more likely to be felt by younger generations, with 62% of Younger Millennials and 63% of Older Millennials claiming to have felt three or more benefits of globalisation.

> **"Younger Millennials show signs of a preference towards British products, with almost a third (31%) agreeing they prefer to purchase British alcoholic drinks for drinking at home, compared to a national average of 22%."**

Ina Mitskavets, Senior Consumer and Lifestyles Analyst at Mintel, said:

"Britain now stands at the intersection of tradition and innovation spurred on by globalised markets, which can be an uncomfortable place for some established domestic businesses. But numerous benefits in the form of lower prices and increased product variety, to name a few, appear to outweigh the short-term pain in the eyes of the consumer."

Topping the list of the benefits of globalisation is technology, with over half (55%) of Brits agreeing that access to cheaper technology products benefits Britain as a country and 51% saying it benefits them personally. Furthermore, cheaper international travel is seen as a benefit to Britain by 50% of UK consumers, whilst 44% agree it benefits them personally.

Whilst these factors are particularly enjoyed as a result of the positive impact on the nation's bank balances, it seems consumers also enjoy the added choice that foreign influences bring. Indeed, availability of both British and international brands in local retailers is seen as a plus, with three in five (59%) agreeing this benefits Britain as a country and two in five (41%) agreeing it benefits them personally. Furthermore, over half (54%) agree that the variety of ethnic restaurants in Britain benefits Britain as a country, whilst 36% say it benefits them personally.

"The personal benefits of globalisation have a more immediate impact on people's finances and well-being. This explains why high proportions of Brits believe that globalisation has given them better access

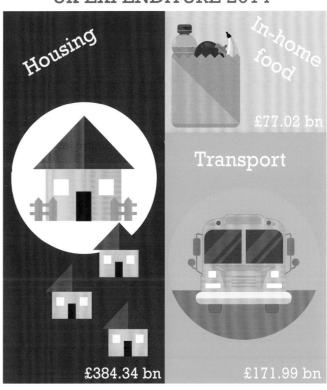

UK EXPENDITURE 2014

Housing £384.34 bn

In-home food £77.02 bn

Transport £171.99 bn

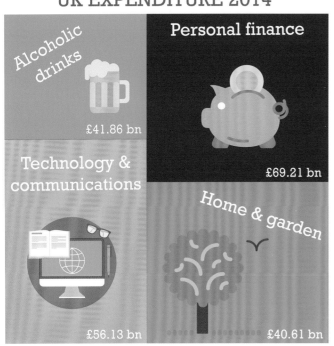

UK EXPENDITURE 2014

Alcoholic drinks £41.86 bn

Personal finance £69.21 bn

Technology & communications £56.13 bn

Home & garden £40.61 bn

to cheaper technology and international travel, whilst many also appreciate availability of both British and foreign brands in shops and a greater variety of ethnic food and drink on supermarket shelves." Ina adds.

"Topping the list of the benefits of globalisation is technology, with over half (55%) of Brits agreeing that access to cheaper technology products benefits Britain as a country and 51% saying it benefits them personally."

Moreover, outside of retail and consumer markets Britons overwhelmingly agree that the influence of globalisation holds benefits for Britain. Four in five (79%) for instance claim that Britain doing business and trading with other countries benefits Britain as a country, whilst 78% say the same of global companies investing in Britain. Additionally, two thirds (66%) say that job opportunities at international companies in Britain benefits the UK, whilst 64% say the same of cultural links between Britain and other countries.

"Whilst Millennials are also developing a taste for British brands and in some cases even matching the enthusiasm of their older counterparts, on the whole, Britishness remains considerably less important to shoppers the younger they are."

Whilst highlighting the positives in globalisation, Mintel's research also found the strong consumer

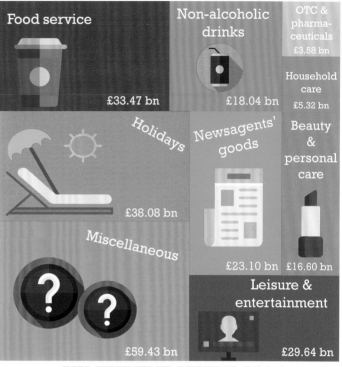

UK EXPENDITURE 2014

Food service £33.47 bn

Non-alcoholic drinks £18.04 bn

OTC & pharmaceuticals £3.58 bn

Household care £5.32 bn

Holidays £38.08 bn

Newsagents' goods £23.10 bn

Beauty & personal care £16.60 bn

Miscellaneous £59.43 bn

Leisure & entertainment £29.64 bn

following for Brand Britain. Over two in five (44%) of Brits agree they prefer buying British brands and products when shopping for food in the home, whilst 28% say they like to buy British fashion and footwear and 26% say they prefer purchasing British furniture and home accessories.

Furthermore, Mintel's research shows that the demand for British products across nearly all categories, bar alcoholic drinks, is driven by the older generations. Three quarters (74%) of the Swing Generation state they prefer buying British food for eating at home, compared to just a third (37%) of Generation X and

Infographics on page 7 and 8 were created based on The Fifty – fifty fascinating markets you need to watch, *by Mintel, 2015.*

Older Millennial consumers. What's more, whilst almost half (45%) of the Swing Generation say they prefer buying British clothing and accessories, just 24% of Older Millennials agree the same.

"Mintel's research shows that the demand for British products across nearly all categories, bar alcoholic drinks, is driven by the older generations. Three quarters (74%) of the Swing Generation state they prefer buying British food for eating at home, compared to just a third (37%) of Generation X and Older Millennial consumers."

"Britishness is especially effective when marketing to older consumers, who put more trust in the quality, safety and value for money they associate with products that are 'Made in the UK'. Perhaps it is simply something that they are used to from childhood, something that provides extra reassurance and comfort."

Younger Millennials, however, do show signs of a preference towards British products, with almost a third (31%) agreeing they prefer to purchase British alcoholic drinks for drinking at home, compared to a national average of 22%. In addition, over a quarter (27%) claim to prefer buying British beauty products and toiletries, a three percentage-point increase on the average of 24% of consumers.

"Whilst Millennials are also developing a taste for British brands and in some cases even matching the enthusiasm of their older counterparts, on the whole, Britishness remains considerably less important to shoppers the younger they are. Retailers therefore should look to the other end of the age spectrum and work out how to balance the needs of consumers from different generations without compromising their bottom line." Ina adds.

Indeed, when questioned on which attributes they associated with British brands and products, good quality came out top with almost three quarters (73%) agreeing with this, whilst safe to use was identified by three in five (58%) and good value for money was picked by half (51%).

"Having basked in the glory of the London Olympics and the Queen's Diamond Jubilee, Brand Britain now needs to figure out how to capitalise on opportunities provided by the increased pace of globalisation and also address the unique challenges open markets present." Ina concludes.

3 June 2015

⇨ The above information is reprinted with kind permission from Mintel. Please visit www.mintel. com for further information.

Did you know?

Globalisation has led to more accessible, and affordable, high-street fashion. Chains like H&M and Zara now sell their goods in many different countries, from Europe to Australia. And if you need evidence of this, you should look no further than the care label inside your clothes. In fact, a journalist for *The Age*, Australia, recently counted a total of seven layers to one of her clothing labels, featuring more than ten different languages!

Source: The downside to globalisation no one warned us about, Lucy Battersby, 19 November 2015. Featured in The Age.

What is the Transatlantic Trade and Investment Partnership?

An article from The Conversation.

THE CONVERSATION

By Christopher Bovis, Professor of Business Law, University of Hull

The Transatlantic Trade and Investment Partnership, or TTIP, will be the world's biggest free trade agreement. It is geared towards increasing trade between the EU and the US by opening various markets currently restricted in access or closed by tariffs or regulatory barriers. These include everything from pharmaceuticals, chemicals and energy to food, drink and clothing.

The deal

Together the US and EU account for around €22 trillion in annual trade, almost half of the world total. By opening trade further, this could boost global GDP by 0.6% a year or more if knock-on effects on productivity are included. And the effects would be even bigger if the deal eliminates permanent trade barriers, such as customs and taxes, which is also being negotiated.

Currently, EU and US businesses pay trade tariffs to sell their products in each other's markets. TTIP would remove these. It would also reduce costs from duplication, where businesses must meet US and EU standards that are often similar but different.

The exact increase in revenues that the deal will bring to specific economies has been debated. Estimates predict that a TTIP deal could increase the size of the EU economy by as much as €120 billion (0.5% of GDP) and the US economy by €95 billion (0.4% of GDP). Supporters on each side emphasise the size of the markets they will be opening up to domestic manufacturers – the EU will gain easier access to 300 million American consumers and vice versa.

But what is the full potential of a free trade agreement between the USA and the EU? This will emerge after the deal is concluded and it is revealed who the winners and losers will be.

What is at stake?

The two biggest obstacles in the ongoing TTIP negotiations relate to the sensitive areas of businesses which verge towards the realms of public policy.

Public services and procurement

Public authorities are major consumers in both Europe and the US. In the EU they spend around €2 trillion annually, equivalent to some 19% of the EU's GDP delivering public services. The US federal procurement spending is approximately US$500 billion per year. Companies on either side want fair access to these markets.

In the UK there are fears that this could put the NHS at risk of US competition. UK ministers and the European Commission have both made guarantees that TTIP would not affect how NHS services are provided, however.

Energy markets and renewable sectors

This is a market in excess of €950 billion annually. TTIP will add liquidity and competition to the energy market, benefiting both EU and US consumers. With renewable energy sources in TTIP negotiations focusing on shale gas, there is the potential for US companies benefiting, as they are already a generation ahead of their EU competition.

Global standards

The most ambitious objective of TTIP is the establishment of global standards in manufacturing products. If progress is achieved towards such objectives, both the EU and US will be winners in liberalising trade.

Certain sectors, such as chemicals and pharmaceuticals will benefit from adopting common standards and authorisation processes. EU firms and the EU pharma sector is expected to gain some advantages over the US competitors, but such advantages could be easily counteracted by public expenditure on health and the processes which relate to intellectual property rights of specialised drugs.

There is more controversy over other areas such as food safety where the US and EU have different standards. Critics argue that the EU has much stricter regulations on GM crops, pesticide use and food additives. They say TTIP could open the EU market to cheaper but poorer quality food.

Democracy and transparency

TTIP negotiations have been criticised for their lack of transparency, with discussions taking place behind closed doors in utmost secrecy.

TTIP also has provisions for introducing "investor-state dispute settlement". This would allow companies to sue foreign governments over claims of unfair treatment, which is detrimental to their profits. Critics say this undermines democracy by giving large companies power to pressure government policies.

Needless to say, TTIP is a huge trade agreement and many of the specifics are yet to be agreed upon. Negotiations started in 2013, but the US at least is determined to close the remaining rounds of negotiations before the term of the current presidency. In the EU, the European Council and the European Parliament must both agree to the outcome of negotiations. The deal must then be separately ratified by the national parliaments of all 28 EU member states.

2 March 2015

⇨ The above information is reprinted with kind permission from *The Conversation*. Please visit www.theconversation.com for further information.

TTIP: the key to freer trade, or corporate greed?

Some say the US/EU trade deal that could be agreed this year will open up markets and promote UK growth. Others fear it will drive down wages and promote privatisation.

By Phillip Inman

Cheap American olive oil could, in a few years' time, be sitting on supermarket shelves next to the Tuscan single estate varieties loved by British foodies. At present a prohibitive tariff on US imports effectively prices them out of contention.

But a groundbreaking trade deal could lower the $1,680-a-tonne tariff on US olive oil to match the $34 a tonne the US charges on imports from the EU. Or the tariffs could disappear altogether. Either way, Greek, Spanish and Italian olive farmers must fear the Transatlantic Trade and Investment Partnership (TTIP), a deal that aims to create a level playing field between them and massive US agri-businesses.

Trade deals were once seen as a panacea for global poverty. In the 1990s, the World Trade Organization was formed to harmonise cross-border regulations on everything from cars to pharmaceuticals and cut tariffs in order to promote the free flow of goods and services around the world.

There was always a fear that, far from being a winning formula for all, lower tariffs would favour the rich and powerful and crucify small producers, who would struggle to compete in an unprotected environment.

The effects of the North American Free Trade Agreement (NAFTA), signed by the US, Mexico and Canada in 1993, appeared to justify that fear: it became in later years a *cause celebre* for anti-poverty campaigners, angered by the plight of Mexican workers. Not only were they subjected to low wages and poor working conditions by newly relocated US corporations – and, as consumers, to the relentless marketing power of Walmart, Coca-Cola and the rest – but the major fringe benefit of cutting corruption remained illusory.

This year the US hopes to sign what many believe will be NAFTA's direct successor – TTIP. Should it get the green light from Congress and the EU commission, the agreement will be a bilateral treaty between Europe and the US, and, just like NAFTA before it, outside the ambit of a gridlocked WTO.

Supporters say it will be an improvement on its predecessor because the main proponents are a liberal US president and a European commission that considers itself concerned with workers and consumers. Why, the commission asks, would 28 relatively affluent member states with concerns about high unemployment, stagnant wages, welfare provision and climate change agree to a charter that undermines workers' rights, attacks public services or reduces environmental regulations?

TTIP is also billed as an agreement between equals that allows both sides to promote trade: it is claimed that the UK's national income could be raised by £4 billion–£10 billion annually, or up to £100 billion over ten years. That amounts to a 0.3 percentage point boost to GDP, which would have pushed this year's expected 2.4% growth to 2.7%.

But it strikes fear into the hearts of many, who believe it to be a Trojan Horse for rapacious corporations. These corporations, hell bent on driving down costs to enhance shareholder value, spell the end for Europe's cosy welfare states and their ability to shield fledgling or, in the case of steel and coal, declining industries from the harsh realities of open competition.

TTIP has been compared to the 1846 Corn Law abolition, which either swept away protectionist tariffs that impoverished millions of workers, or protected a vital source of food and led Karl Marx to ask: "What is free trade under the present condition of society?" His answer was: "It is the freedom which capital has to crush the worker." Is that the case with TTIP? Here are five key factors to consider.

Health and public services

From the moment TTIP became part of President Barack Obama's growth strategy, critics have feared that he little realised the expansionary intentions of US healthcare companies or was too distracted to care. The concern relates to the prospect of EU countries, under pressure from rising healthcare costs, handing over major parts of healthcare provision to the private sector. Once services are in private hands, say critics, TTIP rules will prevent them being taken back into state control.

Since these fears were voiced, trade negotiators have excluded provisions that would have allowed firms to sue governments for the loss of health and public services contracts once they expired. This allows the UK's rail franchise system and the contracting-out of health services to continue under time-limited contracts.

But the US private health industry, which is the largest in the world, views a Europe struggling with the needs of an ageing baby-boomer generation as ripe for the picking. For this reason alone, contracting out the distribution of drugs, the supply of medical devices and the provision of vital services could prove irresistible.

Dispute resolution

A little known facet of every trade deal is a separate form of arbitration for the businesses covered by the agreement, allowing them to avoid the civil courts. As such, the investor-state dispute resolution (ISDS) gives foreign investors the power to sue a government for introducing legislation that harms their investment.

Famously, it was used by Big Tobacco to sue the Australian Government when it introduced plain cigarette packaging. Before and after the scandal, other governments have come under legal challenge from corporations concerned that public policymaking is denying them revenues.

In spring 2014, UN official and human rights lawyer Alfred de Zayas called for a moratorium on TTIP negotiations until investor-state dispute settlement was excluded. He warned that the secret court tribunals held to settle trade disputes were undemocratic. Their reliance on a small group of specialist lawyers also meant that arbitrators sitting in judgement were the ones who at other times represented corporate clients.

De Zayas feared that smaller states would find themselves in the same position as many governments in trade disputes, suffering huge legal bills and long delays to public policy reforms. He was joined in his mission by NGOs and, most importantly, by MEPs in Strasbourg.

As a first concession, the US side agreed to prohibit "brass-plate" firms – those that exist only by name in a county, without any employees or activity – from suing a government. This aimed to prevent a repeat of the Australia incident when the Ukrainian arm of tobacco firm Philip Morris, effectively a brass-plate entity, spearheaded the attack on plain packaging.

Many EU politicians said this concession was too easy to circumvent, leaving corporations in a powerful position. So Europe's chief negotiator, Swedish commissioner Cecilia Malmström, hatched a scheme for an international court of arbitration – an open public forum instead of the private court system. Even her critics said it was a bold move, and unlikely to be accepted by the Americans.

Washington has countered with proposals for a more transparent ISDS court, with live-streamed meetings and the publication of all documents. Not enough, says de Zayas, who wrote recently: "Alas, countless ISDS awards have shown a business bias that shocks the conscience. To the extent that the procedures are not transparent, the arbitrators are not always independent and the annulment procedure is nearly useless, ISDS should be abolished as incompatible with article 14(1) of the ICCPR [International Covenant on Civil and Political Rights] which requires that all suits at law be decided by independent and competent tribunals under the rule of law."

The two sides have yet to formally discuss either proposal: under deals between the US and Japan and the EU and Canada the issue was barely mentioned, but it is now expected to be among the most contentious.

Regulations

Michael Froman, the US chief negotiator, described the task of harmonising regulations as follows: "For years the US and EU have accepted each other's inspection of aeroplanes because it was obvious they would not be able to check all the planes landing in their jurisdiction. We seek to expand this practice to other areas."

So how would Froman apply this to the fact that American cars will still be left-hand drive, restricting their use on British roads? He argues that the cost of

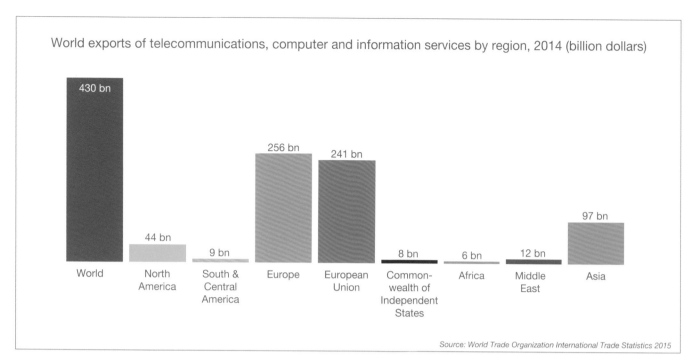

World exports of telecommunications, computer and information services by region, 2014 (billion dollars)

- World: 430 bn
- North America: 44 bn
- South & Central America: 9 bn
- Europe: 256 bn
- European Union: 241 bn
- Commonwealth of Independent States: 8 bn
- Africa: 6 bn
- Middle East: 12 bn
- Asia: 97 bn

Source: World Trade Organization International Trade Statistics 2015

imported cars' research and development and testing can still benefit from the harmonisation of regulations on either side of the Atlantic.

Yet there is nothing US food regulators would like less than to accept processed foods tested by EU officials who failed to spot the horsemeat scandal.

And EU regulators are duty bound to reject GM foods, after sustained protests by Europe's consumers in direct conflict with US farmers. Washington claims it will accept the science when it applies to regulations, which supports GM foods being accepted by the EU as part of TTIP, just as it is part of the WTO agreement.

Tariffs

Dispensing with tariffs seems like a straightforward process compared with tackling complex regulations. Under TTIP, tariffs on goods and services should disappear, though it is expected that some will only be reduced, and others may take years to go the way of history.

Under the Trans-Pacific Partnership (TPP) recently agreed, but not yet implemented, between the US, Japan, Australia, Vietnam and other East Asian countries, all goods, from pork to cars, are covered.

A good example of how long it can take for tariffs to come down is found in the case of the 2.5% rate slapped on Japanese car imports to the US: this will start to be incrementally lowered 15 years after the agreement takes effect, halved in 20 years and eliminated in 25 years. In return, Japan will, among other things, lower its tariff on imported beef from 38.5% to 9% over 16 years. A similar programme could be possible under TTIP, with olive oil tariffs lowered over 25 years.

Labour standards and workers' rights

Japanese trade unions supported the TPP deal, and unions in Europe are expected to follow suit with TTIP.

They accept that labour protection rules lie outside the scope of a deal, and that their governments can therefore continue to implement minimum wage legislation and other supportive measures without being sanctioned.

But unions, where they exist, tend to represent workers in successful industries, which naturally welcome access to wider markets. Workers in weaker areas of the economy could find their jobs coming under pressure from harmonised regulations, lower tariffs, or even just exposure to a US rival with a work ethic that denies most employees more than two weeks' holiday a year.

TTIP is important to the UK Government because the US is our biggest market for goods and services outside the EU. It's seen as especially important for small- and medium-sized businesses, which appreciate the lack of language barrier. Britain also has a trade surplus with the US: we export more than we import, which helps counterbalance the country's huge trade deficit.

Such is the momentum behind the talks that a deal could be agreed by the end of the year, and go before Congress and EU parliaments in 2017. Both sides claim to be making good progress. But the dispute over ISDS and protests from farmers could yet quash Obama's hopes for US olive oil sales.

2 January 2016

⇨ The above information is reprinted with kind permission from *The Guardian*. Please visit www. theguardian.com for further information.

The evolution of trade sanctions

Sanctions used to be a blunt instrument. They aimed to impose costs on the target country with the intention that these costs would lead to a change of behaviour by the targeted government. Since the 1990s, targeted or 'smart' sanctions have been much more popular: the idea was that the costs should be focused on decision makers rather than on the general population, or they should be targeted at a particular activity that the sanctioning countries want to stop. This led to a proliferation of different types of sanction.

1.1 Targeted sanctions

Sanctions that target individuals have become increasingly popular in recent years. These measures are applied to individuals, usually powerful figures connected with a government whose policy great powers (it is usually the more powerful states that create sanctions regimes) want to change, and entities: usually companies associated with those governments. Targeted (or 'smart') sanctions are also applied to organisations and individuals who have been designated as 'terrorist'. They usually include travel bans and asset freezes and may include bans on trading with companies or bans on those companies from financial markets. Targeted sanctions can also include trade bans on particular goods or economic sectors. These can aim to constrain a particular activity directly. Targeted sanctions are intended to do less damage to the wellbeing of ordinary citizens in the sanctioned country, The sanctions regime against Saddam Hussein's government in Iraq came in for criticism for damaging the lives and health of Iraqis: "clearly a humanitarian disaster". This sort of sanction should also do less damage to the economies of countries applying the sanctions.

1.2 Financial sanctions

Globalisation has increased the importance of Western, particularly US, financial markets; restricting access to Western finance is a significant tool. Access to financial markets has been cut off as a means to apply pressure to Russia and Iran, as well as in other cases. Financial sanctions usually fall somewhere between targeted sanctions and broader measures; they are often applied to some but not all financial institutions in the target country. The US imposed financial sanctions on North Korea in 2005, adding to an aid and trade embargo that had been in place for some time. It turned out that the financial sanctions were a major blow to the North Korean Government; far more effective than the regime that had been in place, and more effective than expected by the US administration.

1.3 Trade sanctions

Broad trade sanctions are sometimes referred to as 'tier three' sanctions. They are often the last type of measure to be applied because they are undoubtedly a blunt instrument that will affect the livelihoods of ordinary people in the target country and do broad damage to the country applying the sanction. The ban on the import of Iranian oil is a well-known example of a broad trade sanction.

1.4 Diplomatic sanctions and aid

Some people include among sanctions diplomatic measures such as downgrading diplomatic relations or excluding a country from the meetings of international groups such as the G20. The suspension of aid can also be considered a sanction. This has been particularly important in such countries as Zimbabwe. In December 2012, the UK (along with other donors) suspended all budget support to the Ugandan Government in response to corruption within the Prime Minister's Office.

1.5 Multilateral and unilateral sanctions

Most UK sanctions regimes are set up in collaboration with other member states in the EU, many are coordinated at the higher level of the United Nations. There is a clear advantage if many countries agree to apply sanctions: their impact will be much greater. The EU has shown an increasing willingness to impose sanctions that are not backed by or go further than the provisions of a UN Security Council resolution. However, there are also drawbacks to multilateral sanctions. The US has often sought to impose sanctions unilaterally because the long and often fractious negotiating process in agreeing multilateral sanctions means that they may be later and weaker than the US Government wants. With the world's largest economy and, particularly, financial centre, the US can impose effective sanctions unilaterally. If a smaller country such as the UK did this, it would have less impact.

5 June 2015

⇨ The above information is reprinted with kind permission from parliament.uk. Please visit their website for further information.

UKTI reveals record number of UK businesses looking to export

Figures show a record number of UK businesses are interested in exporting through the Government's Exporting is GREAT website.

New figures today (18 April 2016) show a record number of UK businesses interested in exporting through government-brokered opportunities, with over 20,000 responses since November 2015. The news comes as the Government kicks off Exporting is GREAT Week.

The statistics, released by UK Trade and Investment (UKTI) the government department leading Exporting is GREAT, demonstrate the huge demand for UK products and services overseas. Over 6,000 export opportunities have been showcased at exportingisgreat.gov.uk since November 2015. This equates to 40 new opportunities every day or a new chance to export roughly every 37 minutes for UK businesses.

Opportunities have come from 109 countries and 44 different sectors, including the chance to sell tea to China or cheese to France. They also highlight a Spanish demand for our deckchairs and a Finnish thirst for British beer.

Trade and Investment Minister, Lord Price, said:

"We have a proud history as a trading nation. The development of digital technology has the potential to give even the smallest company a global reach and access to attractive new markets.

"This Government is committed to supporting 100,000 more UK businesses to export by 2020. Exporting is GREAT Week is the perfect time to inspire companies to take advantage of the world of opportunity out there and the global demand for British products, skills and expertise."

> **"We have a proud history as a trading nation. The development of digital technology has the potential to give even the smallest company a global reach and access to attractive new markets."**

Today's figures are revealed on the first day of Exporting is GREAT Week. Running from 18 to 22 April 2016, the week sees around 90 events take place across the UK to help more first-time exporters make exporting work for them. Companies are increasingly realising the benefits of strengthening their overseas business, with new exporters making up nearly a fifth of UKTI customers (19%).

In addition, since November 2015, as part of a year-long roadshow around the UK, the Exporting is GREAT Export Hub, has provided close to 3,000 companies with advice and support to grow their business overseas and brought them face-to-face with live global export opportunities.

UK Export Finance (UKEF) can also provide financial advice for companies of all sizes. The UK's export credit agency helps businesses to realise export opportunities through guidance from a specialist export finance adviser and through insurance and bank guarantees to support export contracts.

Over the past five years, UKEF has provided over £17 billion worth of support to British businesses – helping more than 300 businesses directly and many thousands more in their supply chains.

18 April 2016

⇨ The above information is reprinted with kind permission from the Department for International Trade, UK Export Finance and Lord Price. Please visit GOV.UK for further information.

Fair trade myths and FAQs

As awareness of fair trade grows, so do misconceptions. These are some popular myths about fair trade and the realities behind them.

Myth: Fair trade is about paying developed world wages in the developing world

Reality: Wages are designed to provide fair compensation based on the true cost of production, and are not based on North American wage standards.

Fair wages are determined by a number of factors, including:

⇨ The amount of time, skill, and effort involved in production

⇨ Minimum and living wages where products are made

⇨ The purchasing power in a community or area

⇨ Other costs of living in the local context.

Myth: Fair trade siphons off American jobs to other countries

Reality: Fair trade seeks to improve the lives of the poorest of the poor who frequently lack alternative sources of income. Most fair trade craft products stem from cultures and traditions which are not represented in North American production. Most fair trade food products do not have North American-based alternatives.

Also, as North American fair trade organisations grow as successful small businesses, they employ more and more individuals in their communities.

Myth: Fair trade is anti-globalisation

Reality: international exchange lies at the heart of fair trade. 360° fair trade organisations seek to maximise the positive elements of globalisation that connect people, communities and cultures through products and ideas. At the same time, they seek to minimise the negative elements that result in lower labour, social and environmental standards which hide the true costs of production.

Myth: Fair trade is a form of charity

Reality: 360° fair trade promotes positive and long-term change through trade-based relationships which build self-sufficiency. Its success depends on independent, successfully-run organisations and businesses – not on handouts. While many fair trade organisations support charitable projects in addition to their work in trade, the exchange of goods remains the key element of their work.

Myth: Fair trade results in more expensive goods for the consumer

Reality: most fair trade products are competitively priced in relation to their conventional counterparts. 360° fair trade organisations work directly with producers, cutting out middlemen, so they can keep products affordable for consumers and return a greater percentage of the price to the producers.

Myth: Fair trade results in low-quality products for the consumer

Reality: while handmade products naturally include some variation, 360° fair trade organisations continuously work to improve quality and consistency. Through direct and long-term relationships, producers and fair trade organisations dialogue about consumer needs and create high-quality products. Fair traders have received awards at the international Cup of Excellence and Roaster of the Year competitions, SustainAbility in Design, the New York Home Textile Show and other venues.

Myth: Fair trade refers only to coffee and chocolate

Reality: Fair trade encompasses a wide variety of agricultural and handcrafted goods, including baskets, clothing, cotton, home and kitchen decor, jewellery, rice, soap, tea, toys, and wine. While coffee was the first agricultural product to be certified fair trade in 1988, fair trade handcrafts have been sold since 1946.

FAQs

What does 'fair' really mean?

The word 'fair' can mean a lot of different things to different people. Fair trade is about more than just paying a fair wage. It means that trading partnerships are based on reciprocal benefits and mutual respect; that prices paid to producers reflect the work they do; that producers share decision-making power; that national health, safety and wage laws are enforced; and that products are environmentally sustainable and conserve natural resources.

How do I know that a product is fair trade?

The Fair Trade Federation screens and verifies companies that practise

360° fair trade. These organisations don't just buy and sell a few fair trade products; they integrate fair trade practices into everything they do. These organisations have a deep level of commitment to fair trade practices and maintain long-term relationships with small producer organisations.

You will also see some products in the marketplace that carry a fair trade certification seal. Fair trade certification involves a worksite audit and a 10% fair trade premium. These labels increasingly focus on large factories and farms. They are often used by multinational brands who cannot be fully fair trade but wish to improve some of their practices.

Do fair trade goods cost more than comparable non-fair trade goods?

Generally, goods sold by 360° Fair Trade Organizations cost the same or a few percent more than similar quality, conventional goods. These fair trade products don't cost more because the large percentage taken by middle people is removed from the equation. The cost remains the same as conventionally traded goods; however, more of the sale price goes to producers.

In the case of agricultural goods, is the quality comparable to conventional products?

In some cases the quality is actually higher because fair trade organizations factor in the environmental cost of production. For instance, in the case of coffee, fairly traded coffee is often organic and shade grown, which results in a higher quality coffee.

What is a fair wage?

Producers receive a fair wage when they are paid fairly for their products. This means that workers are paid a living wage, which enables them to cover basic needs, including food, shelter, education and healthcare for their families. Paying fair wages does not necessarily mean that products cost the consumer more. 360° fair trade organisations bypass exploitative middle people and work directly with producers.

How much money (per cent of sale price) do the artisans make?

Living wages vary widely between regions of the world and individual communities. Therefore, there is no set percentage given to artisans. Rather, open communication ensures that pricing is transparent and meets the full needs of artisans. A 360° fair trade relationship is a true partnership, allowing all to make a fair profit margin.

Why do 360° fair trade organisations support cooperative workplaces?

Cooperatives and producer associations provide a healthy alternative to large-scale manufacturing and sweatshop conditions, where unprotected workers earn below minimum wage and most of the profits flow to foreign investors and local elites who have little interest in ensuring the long-term health of the communities in which they work. 360° fair trade organisations work with small businesses, worker-owned and democratically run cooperatives and associations which bring significant benefits to workers and their communities. By banding together, workers are able to access credit, reduce raw material costs and establish higher and more just prices for their products. Workers earn a greater return on their labour, and profits are distributed more equitably and often reinvested in community projects such as health clinics, childcare, education and literacy training. Workers learn important leadership and organising skills, enabling self-reliant grassroots-driven development.

How do 360° fair trade organisations offer financial support to producers?

Small-scale farmers and artisans in the developing world lack access to affordable financing, impeding their profitability. 360° fair trade organisations buy products directly from producers and provide advance payment or pre-harvest financing. Unlike many commercial importers who often wait 60–90 days before paying producers, 360° fair trade organisations ensure pre-payment so that producers have sufficient funds to cover raw materials and basic needs during production.

How do 360° fair trade organisations offer technical support to producers?

360° fair trade organisations provide critical technical assistance and support such as market information, organisational development and training in financial management. Unlike conventional importers, 360° fair trade organisations establish long-term relationships with their producers and help them adapt production to changing trends.

Note: some of the information above was originally published by the Fair Trade Resource Network.

⇨ The above information is reprinted with kind permission from the Fair Trade Federation. Please visit www.fairtradefederation.org for further information.

What is the World Trade Organization?

The World Trade Organization (WTO) is the only global international organisation dealing with the rules of trade between nations. At its heart are the WTO agreements, negotiated and signed by the bulk of the world's trading nations and ratified in their parliaments. The goal is to help producers of goods and services, exporters, and importers conduct their business.

Who we are

There are a number of ways of looking at the World Trade Organization. It is an organisation for trade opening. It is a forum for governments to negotiate trade agreements. It is a place for them to settle trade disputes. It operates a system of trade rules. Essentially, the WTO is a place where member governments try to sort out the trade problems they face with each other.

The WTO was born out of negotiations, and everything the WTO does is the result of negotiations. The bulk of the WTO's current work comes from the 1986–94 negotiations called the Uruguay Round and earlier negotiations under the General Agreement on Tariffs and Trade (GATT). The WTO is currently the host to new negotiations, under the 'Doha Development Agenda' launched in 2001.

Where countries have faced trade barriers and wanted them lowered, the negotiations have helped to open markets for trade. But the WTO is not just about opening markets, and in some circumstances its rules support maintaining trade barriers – for example, to protect consumers or prevent the spread of disease.

At its heart are the WTO agreements, negotiated and signed by the bulk of the world's trading nations. These documents provide the legal ground rules for international commerce. They are essentially contracts, binding governments to keep their trade policies within agreed limits. Although negotiated and signed by governments, the goal is to help producers of goods and services, exporters and importers conduct their business, while allowing governments to meet social and environmental objectives.

The system's overriding purpose is to help trade flow as freely as possible – so long as there are no undesirable side effects – because this is important for economic development and well-being. That partly means removing obstacles. It also means ensuring that individuals, companies and governments know what the trade rules are around the world, and giving them the confidence that there will be no sudden changes of policy. In other words, the rules have to be 'transparent' and predictable.

Trade relations often involve conflicting interests. Agreements, including those painstakingly negotiated in the WTO system, often need interpreting. The most harmonious way to settle these differences is through some neutral procedure based on an agreed legal foundation. That is the purpose behind the dispute settlement process written into the WTO agreements.

What we do

The WTO is run by its member governments. All major decisions are made by the membership as a whole, either by ministers (who usually meet at least once every two years) or by their ambassadors or delegates (who meet regularly in Geneva).

While the WTO is driven by its member states, it could not function without its Secretariat to coordinate the activities. The Secretariat employs over 600 staff, and its experts – lawyers, economists, statisticians and communications experts – assist WTO members on a daily basis to ensure, among other things, that negotiations progress smoothly, and that the rules of international trade are correctly applied and enforced.

Trade negotiations

The WTO agreements cover goods, services and intellectual property. They spell out the principles of liberalisation, and the permitted exceptions. They include individual countries' commitments to lower customs tariffs and other trade barriers, and to open, and keep open, services markets. They set procedures for settling disputes. These agreements are not static; they are renegotiated from time to time and new agreements can be added to the package. Many are now being negotiated under the Doha Development Agenda, launched by WTO trade ministers in Doha, Qatar, in November 2001.

Implementation and monitoring

WTO agreements require governments to make their trade policies transparent by notifying the WTO about laws in force and measures adopted. Various WTO councils and committees seek to ensure that these requirements are being followed and that WTO agreements are being properly implemented. All WTO members must undergo periodic scrutiny of their trade policies and practices, each review containing reports by the country concerned and the WTO Secretariat.

Dispute settlement

The WTO's procedure for resolving trade quarrels under the Dispute Settlement Understanding is vital for enforcing the rules and therefore for ensuring that trade flows smoothly. Countries bring disputes to the WTO if they think their rights under the agreements are being infringed. Judgements by specially appointed independent experts are based on interpretations of the agreements and individual countries' commitments.

Building trade capacity

WTO agreements contain special provision for developing countries, including longer time periods to implement agreements and commitments, measures to increase their trading opportunities, and support to help them build their trade capacity, to handle disputes and to implement technical standards. The WTO organises hundreds of technical cooperation missions to developing countries annually. It also holds numerous courses each year in Geneva for government officials. Aid for Trade aims to help developing countries develop the skills and infrastructure needed to expand their trade.

Outreach

The WTO maintains regular dialogue with non-governmental organisations, parliamentarians, other international organisations, the media and the general public on various aspects of the WTO and the ongoing Doha negotiations, with the aim of enhancing cooperation and increasing awareness of WTO activities.

⇨ The above information is reprinted with kind permission from the World Trade Organization. Please visit www.wto.org for further information.

World Trade Organization 2016

Major exporters and importers of personal, cultural and recreational services, 2013 and 2014 (million dollars and percentage)							
	Value		Share in ten economies		Annual percentage change		
	2013	2014	2013	2010–13	2012	2013	2014
Exporters							
European Union	29,838	28,989	75.8	12	2	19	-3
Canada	2,927	2,448	7.4	19	19	1	-16
Turkey	1,286	1,796	3.3	-4	-4	5	40
India	1,232	1,266	3.1	123	123	61	3
Russian Federation	770	681	2.0	13	13	39	-12
Korea, Republic of	731	955	1.9	30	30	8	31
Australia	722	882	1.8	4	4	-20	22
United States	714	747	1.8	9	9	-20	5
Switzerland	606	770	1.5	-5	-5	56	27
Singapore	543	550	1.4	3	3	2	1

Source: World Trade Organization International Trade Statistics 2015

Britain fails to understand the nature of globalisation at its peril

An article from The Conversation.

THE CONVERSATION

By Jennifer Johns, Senior Lecturer in International Business and Economic Geography, University of Liverpool

There remains great uncertainty in the aftermath of the UK vote to leave the European Union. Few seem to have a plan for what Brexit will look like and how the UK's relationship with the outside world will take shape.

But while the desire for sovereignty and to "take back control" were top of many voters' list of reasons to vote to leave, the fact that we live in a globalised world where economies and trade supersede national boundaries cannot be ignored.

Much of the confusion about how Brexit will affect the British economy has resulted from the inability of those for and against it to acknowledge the realities of the position of the UK in the contemporary global economy. This failure to understand the realities of globalisation is partly why there is such confusion about how to deliver the kind of post-Brexit UK demanded by those who voted leave. But regaining national sovereignty is extremely difficult, if not impossible, in today's global economy.

The interconnected world

The recent global financial crisis should have sent a powerful message. The degree of interconnection between places in the global economy has reached unprecedented levels and attempts to "unpick" these interconnections are highly problematic.

Globalisation is complex. It is no longer a case of "us" and "them". Capital, goods and services flow within, between and across national borders – and the flow is uneven. It is often directed through key cities. So when we talk about flows of foreign direct investment between the UK and Germany, we are actually discussing flows of people and money between cities such as London and Berlin.

In fact, cities are the key drivers in trade. It is no surprise therefore that there were significantly higher votes to remain in the EU in cities such as London and Manchester. This is because these cities are points in the global economy through which trade, services and people flow. It is in these locations that we can most easily see the benefits of interconnection with cities in the EU and beyond.

Outside of the major cities, the regions of the UK have experienced a downward shift in the scale at which economic activity takes place and political power is exercised. The national shift from manufacturing to a service-based economy has had a geographically uneven impact. Many manufacturing industries in the UK's regions have shrunk or disappeared. This has not been helped by UK national policy which focuses on the financial services sector (predominately in London).

Globalisation's disconnect

Globalisation has brought with it disconnection between the way that economies and their management have been simultaneously downscaled and upscaled. So, as well as the concentration of decision making in Westminster, there are also a number of decisions being made abroad that affect regions across the UK – the evolution of the European Union epitomises this process.

This upscaling of power is necessary. Many of the most

important issues of the last three decades are shared across national boundaries – take for example environmental concerns. The formation of supra-regions begins with an acknowledgement of the benefits of removing trade barriers and having free movement of goods and services, which should create opportunities for all regions of the UK.

In fact, the best hope for deprived areas of the UK is not to place decision making squarely back in the hands of the UK Government. This gives power back to the very institutions that created and exacerbated the regional inequalities seen in the UK today. Benefits such as investment in local enterprises and infrastructure, improvements in working conditions and levels of employment result from international engagement and cooperation.

Those who – justifiably – feel isolated and economically depressed should call for greater decision-making power at a more local level. Local power, combined with access to international resources and opportunities, can start rebuilding local economies. Globalisation makes this possible as cities and regions do not necessarily need to go via London for trade and investment. These connections are essential for local economies to compete in the globalised world.

But leaving the EU means leaving the hundreds of trade agreements the UK has with non-EU countries and also possibly the freedom of movement of goods and services there is within the EU. Until these are rearranged (which will take several decades), the UK's constituent regions may struggle to access international markets. So the "take back control" rhetoric offers no solutions, only problems.

The UK Government has consistently failed to articulate the rationale and benefits of upscaling in its relations globally (specifically in the form of EU membership), despite the economic benefits it has brought. It is not about the removal of national boundaries but rather an acceptance of how so much of what drives the global economy occurs outside of these strict boundaries.

Closer economic cooperation is the only logical response to globalisation and the best way to ensure stable growth. Indeed, the short-, medium- and long-term impacts of the Brexit vote will surely serve to provide the UK with a harsh lesson in the dangers of going it alone.

5 August 2016

⇨ The above information is reprinted with kind permission from *The Conversation*. Please visit www.theconversation.com for further information.

Change in UK three-monthly trade with significant partner countries, May to July 2016 compared with February to April 2016					
	Exports (£ million)			Imports (£ million)	
	May to July 2016 value	Three-monthly change		May to July 2016 value	Three-monthly change
1. USA	11,343	-257	1. Germany	15949	+283
2. Germany	7,962	+6	2. China	10870	+1367
3. The Netherlands	4,633	+79	3. USA	9366	+240
4. France	4,932	+75	4. The Netherlands	8582	+157
5. Republic of Ireland	4,356	+360	5. France	6317	+151
6. China	3,567	-941	6. Belgium and Luxembourg	5946	+176
7. Belgium and Luxembourg	3,009	+131	7. Italy	4275	+54
8. Switzerland	1,553	-92	8. Spain	4122	+261
9. Spain	2,268	-9	9. Republic of Ireland	3235	+59
10. Italy	2,407	+70	10. Norway	3146	+251

Source: Office for National Statistics, July 2016

Notes:

1. Significant trading partners defined as top 10 export markets and import sources 2015.

2. USA includes Puerto Rico.

UK aid: tackling global challenges in the national interest

Foreword from the report by HM Treasury and the Department for International Development.

Britain will continue to meet its commitments on aid spending.

We firmly believe that spending 0.7% of Gross National Income (GNI) on international development – alongside our commitment to spend 2% on defence – means our country walking taller in the world.

Over the last five years, UK aid has reached millions across the world. We have supported 11 million children through school. We have distributed 47 million bed nets, contributing to malaria deaths falling by 60% over the last 15 years. And we have supported over 60 million people to access clean water, better sanitation or improved hygiene conditions.

We recognise, however, that aid spending has sometimes been controversial at home, because people want to know that it is squarely in the UK's national interest.

Recent crises have proved, though, why aid is so important for us as well as for the countries we assist. From our response to the Ebola epidemic to our use of our aid budget to lead the international community in responding to the refugee crisis on Europe's borders, it is clear that strategic aid spending can command widespread support.

So we have used the *2015 Spending Review* to fundamentally review how this budget is spent.

This strategy outlines our new approach to aid spending that we believe will command public confidence. The world is changing, and our strategy on aid needs to change with it.

So our aid budget will be restructured to ensure that it is spent on tackling the great global challenges – from the root causes of mass migration and disease, to the threat of terrorism and global climate change – all of which also directly threaten British interests.

We want to meet our promises to the world's poor and also put international development at the heart of our national security and foreign policy.

In line with that principle, we will shape our spending according to four strategic objectives. They are:

Strengthening global peace, security and governance: the Government will invest more to tackle the causes of instability, insecurity and conflict, and to tackle crime and corruption. This is fundamental to poverty reduction overseas, and will also strengthen our own national security at home.

Strengthening resilience and response to crises: this includes more support for ongoing crises including that in Syria and other countries in the Middle East and North Africa region, more science and technology spend on global public health risks such as antimicrobial resistance, and support for efforts to mitigate and adapt to climate change.

Promoting global prosperity: the Government will use Official Development Assistance (ODA) to promote economic development and prosperity in the developing world. This will contribute to the reduction of poverty and also strengthen UK trade and investment opportunities around the world.

Tackling extreme poverty and helping the world's most vulnerable: the Government will strive to eliminate extreme poverty by 2030, and support the world's poorest people to ensure that every person has access to basic needs, including prioritising the rights of girls and women. This will build security, stability and opportunity that will benefit us all.

We will achieve our manifesto commitments in full, including getting 11 million children into school, helping 60 million get access to clean water and sanitation, saving 1.4 million children's lives through immunisations, and improving nutrition for at least 50 million people.

We also recognise that badly spent aid betrays both the countries we should be helping and the taxpayers whose money it is. We made significant progress over the last parliament to drive value for money through all our development spending. But there is always more to do. So we have put in place clear processes to drive

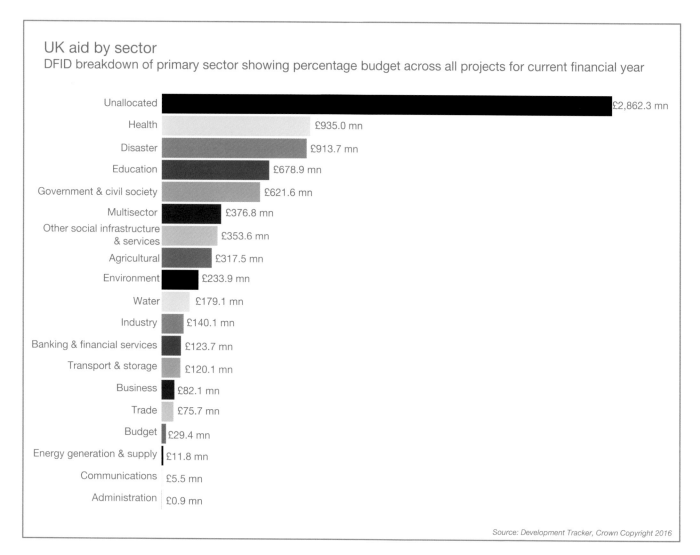

UK aid by sector

DFID breakdown of primary sector showing percentage budget across all projects for current financial year

Unallocated	£2,862.3 mn
Health	£935.0 mn
Disaster	£913.7 mn
Education	£678.9 mn
Government & civil society	£621.6 mn
Multisector	£376.8 mn
Other social infrastructure & services	£353.6 mn
Agricultural	£317.5 mn
Environment	£233.9 mn
Water	£179.1 mn
Industry	£140.1 mn
Banking & financial services	£123.7 mn
Transport & storage	£120.1 mn
Business	£82.1 mn
Trade	£75.7 mn
Budget	£29.4 mn
Energy generation & supply	£11.8 mn
Communications	£5.5 mn
Administration	£0.9 mn

Source: Development Tracker, Crown Copyright 2016

value for money and systematically identify poor-quality spending, and have reviewed all existing spending. As a result, we have ended projects which were not delivering value for money or which were not in line with our objectives.

The strategy sets out how, as a result of our new approach, we will:

⇨ allocate 50% of all DFID's spending to fragile states and regions;

⇨ increase aid spending for the Syrian crisis and the related region;

⇨ end all traditional general budget support – so we can better target spending;

⇨ use an expanded cross-government Conflict, Stability and Security Fund (CSSF) to underpin our security objectives by supporting the international work of the National Security Council (NSC);

⇨ create a £500-million ODA crisis reserve to allow still greater flexibility to respond to emerging crises such as the displacement of Syrian refugees;

⇨ fund a new £1-billion commitment to global public health (the "Ross Fund") which will fund work to tackle the most dangerous infectious diseases, including malaria. The fund will also support work to fight diseases of epidemic potential, such as Ebola, neglected tropical diseases and drug-resistant infections, and use a new cross-government Prosperity Fund, led by the NSC, to drive forward our aim of promoting global prosperity.

We believe this fundamental shift in how we use 0.7% of our national income will show there is no distinction between reducing poverty, tackling global challenges and serving our national interest – all are inextricably linked.

We will ensure that every penny of money spent delivers value for taxpayers, and projects that do not will be cancelled.

With this new strategy, Britain can be proud to be a country that not only meets its responsibilities to the world's poorest, but in doing so best serves and protects its own security and interests.

November 2015

⇨ The above information is reprinted with kind permission from HM Treasury and the Department for International Development. Please visit www.gov.uk for further information.

It's not your father's globalisation any more

Globalisation has morphed in a very different – and more digital – direction, writes James Manyika on LinkedIn.

By James Manyika

It's no surprise that globalisation, always a hot-button topic, has resurfaced in the US presidential race. But a lot of the discussion continues to re-litigate the past rather than proposing how to compete in the future. While we're still talking about tariffs, trade deficits and currency wars, globalisation has morphed in a very different – and more digital – direction.

Our old image of globalisation was one of container ships moving manufactured goods from far-flung factories to markets around the world. Cross-border trade in goods remains a major force in the global economy, but the world's web of economic connections has grown deeper, broader and more intricate.

Now a multinational energy giant can monitor production remotely by installing sensors on 4,000 oil wells around the world. A manufacturer in Australia that needs components can find them from a Chinese supplier on Alibaba – or 3D print them from a digital design file transmitted from Europe. Adele can introduce a song on YouTube and sell millions of downloads in a matter of days. The girl in Kenya who logs on for a personalised math lesson from the California-based Khan Academy is part of the story, too. So are the thousands of Syrian refugees who turn to Facebook for updates to guide their journey to safety.

New research from the McKinsey Global Institute looks at how all types of global flows influence economic growth. We find that over the course of a decade, cross-border flows of goods, services, finance, people, and data increased world GDP by roughly ten per cent over what would have occurred in a world without any flows. This value was equivalent to $7.8 trillion in 2014 alone.

What really jumps out from our findings is that data flows account for $2.8 trillion of this effect. Not only do they represent a stream of communication, transactions, ideas, and information with tremendous value in their own right, but they also play a role in enabling other, more traditional types of flows. When we consider both of these effects together, data flows now have a larger impact on economic growth than the global goods trade – pretty remarkable when you consider that the world's trade networks took centuries to develop but cross-border data flows barely registered just 15 years ago.

This shift creates an opening for countries to redefine their roles in the global economy. The United States is still a major engine of global consumer demand for imported goods. But now it's also the world's leading producer of digital platforms and content. In fact, it accounts for more than 50 per cent

It's hard to compete with cheap imports.

IMPORTS

Local Fabrics

Cheer up; I've just sold half of our stock of fabrics on Facebook!

EXPORTS

of online content consumed in every region of the world except Europe. The United States found itself at a disadvantage in a world where low labour costs were the most important factor in the equation, but digital globalisation plays directly to its strengths in technology and innovation.

"Over the course of a decade, cross-border flows of goods, services, finance, people and data increased world GDP by roughly ten per cent over what would have occurred in a world without any flows. This value was equivalent to $7.8 trillion in 2014 alone."

This doesn't mean that the developing world will necessarily be left behind. Previous MGI research found that the biggest benefits of traditional trade flows go to countries at the centre of the global network. But our latest report finds that countries at the periphery of digital networks stand to gain even more than those at the centre. Companies based in developing countries can overcome constraints in their local markets and connect with global customers, suppliers, financing, and talent. For economies that have been relatively disconnected, the arrival of new digital platforms and cross-border data flows can be transformational.

It's true that all types of global flows remain heavily concentrated among a handful of advanced economies, but digital platforms open the door for developing countries, small businesses and billions of individuals around the world to participate. E-commerce marketplaces such as Alibaba, Amazon, eBay, Flipkart and Rakuten, for example, are turning millions of small enterprises around the world into exporters. Facebook estimates that 50 million small businesses are on its platform, up from 25 million in 2013; on average 30 per cent of their fans are from other countries.

As digital globalisation takes hold, we are entering some uncharted territory. Companies will be challenged to devise business models that can monetise digital consumption. Industry value chains and supply chains could evolve in unexpected ways if 3D printing is widely adopted. Even our old methods of measuring and tracking what moves across borders will have to change.

There are also hopeful signs that the new digital globalisation is not a zero-sum game. One country's participation in digital flows doesn't have to come at another's expense; it can increase economic growth across the board. Now more than ever before, companies and countries can't afford to ignore the opportunities beyond their own borders.

25 February 2016

⇨ The above information is reprinted with kind permission from McKinsey & Company. Please visit www.mckinsey.com for further information.

Trade Winds: shaping the future of international business

Executive summary.

This report explores how international business has changed over 150 years and what may come next. It aims to provide practical insight and considerations for the business leaders we work with around the world. In tracing history and then looking forward, we have identified four key factors – or trade winds – that are a constant and significant presence:

⇨ The march of industrialisation

⇨ The plummeting cost of transport and logistics

⇨ Liberalisation of trade policy

⇨ The evolution of company operating models

⇨ The need for trade.

Saudi Arabia is the world's largest producer of oil but it is not self-sufficient. If its residents want to buy cars, the country must trade with countries such as Japan, the United States and Germany. Trade arises because countries differ in their abilities to produce the goods and services demanded by their citizens. The uneven global distribution of natural resources, capital stock (factories, machinery, equipment) and skilled labour force drives supply and demand around the world. As economies evolve, what they trade evolves too, from exporting natural resources and raw materials to selling high value-added products and services. This activity then increases the value of a nation's economic position.

Historians have distinguished two significant periods of rapid trade expansion – what we refer to as waves of globalisation – over the past 150 years. The first began in the second half of the 19th century and lasted until the outbreak of the Great War. The second started after World War II and lasted until the recent global financial crisis. Although growth in trade volumes has been lacklustre in recent years, our analysis provides reasons for optimism that growth will pick up over the next few years, allowing a third wave of globalisation to unfold that will continue to revolutionise the global economic landscape.

Wave one: 1865–1913

Looking back to 1865, Britain was the world's dominant global powerhouse, leading the way through the Industrial Revolution that in a short timeframe saw it reverse the direction of textile trading with India, import refrigerated foodstuffs from as far afield as Australia, and form the basis of an open market with wider Europe. In this first wave of globalisation, the value of merchandise trade increased fivefold, from US$67 billion in 1865 to US$310 billion and spread through Europe and to the US. But this pace of expansion slowed abruptly during the two world wars and Great Depression of the early twentieth century, which undermined the process of globalisation for several decades.

Wave two: 1950–2007

After World War II global power shifted further west, with the US taking pole position and opening up a 'Golden Age' of prosperity. Consumers discovered new tastes for foreign goods, and their demands created huge opportunities for economies such as Japan and the US to export everything from cars to washing machines and televisions – a new form of industrialisation. Trade liberalisation came to the fore after World War II with governments across the globe keen to embrace new ways of working together for the greater good. The cost of transportation continued to plummet, bringing down barriers to exporting. After a temporary slowdown in the expansion of global trade in the 1970s linked to the oil crises of this period, a number of developing economies in Asia seized the opportunity to jump-start their process of industrialisation and fuel the expansion of their economies through export-led growth. By the 1990s, the age of hyperglobalisation was born, with a new generation of multinational companies being created to take advantage of an increasingly interconnected

world to develop global supply chains. These companies deployed new operating models (e.g. platform-based, collaborative models) that acted as a huge driving force for growth in this period, and while this momentum slowed in the subsequent recession of the 2000s, they will continue to play a significant role in coming years. In this second wave of globalisation, the value of merchandise trade increased more than 30-fold from US$450 billion in 1950 to US$14.6 trillion by 2007.

Wave three: today–2050

Global trade volumes have disappointed recently, but our projections indicate that an upturn in growth may be just around the corner. Although there remains downside risks to the outlook, the next few years should carry the global economy into the next wave of globalisation, critically underpinned by sophisticated and pervasive digital technology that reduces international trade barriers, improves communication between cultures, levels the playing field for entrepreneurs and start ups, and forms the foundation for an 'always-on' global economy. Our projections show that world trade is expected to quadruple in value to reach $68.5 trillion of goods traded each year by 2050. The world market and patterns of trade may look very different by then as shifting demographics and economics catch up – there will be almost three billion new members of the middle class by 2050, most of whom will be located in emerging markets. Still, growth will continue to be driven by the same four trade winds that carried the first traders across the open sea.

The march of industrialisation:

In the third wave of globalisation, mass production will shift to mass customisation. Companies must consider how to develop products and services that are hyper-localised. Some companies have already embraced the concept of reverse innovation, where products and services are developed first in the emerging world and then brought to the developed economies. Executives must reconsider how and where items are being produced, and an optimal global value chain that serves the specific needs of regional customers.

Plummeting transport and logistics costs:

Consider how improved global connectivity and the lower cost of transport/logistics could lead to working with new partners in new countries which may benefit business and the economy. For example, sensors and radio frequency identification device tags are still expensive today, but their rapid adoption will ultimately lead to lower costs, safer handling of goods and significant reduction in spoilage and waste. China's One Belt, One Road project and its Asia Infrastructure Investment Bond initiative also hold the promise of supporting infrastructure spending in Asia and thereby lowering transport costs in the region.

Liberalisation of trade policy:

Open markets can be good for everyone – not only do they bring new goods and services to an untapped market, but they lead to greater economic development and better quality of life. Executives should push for more liberal trade policies to drive continued business and macroeconomic growth.

The evolution of company operating models:

Traditional ways of conducting business will evolve over the next several decades, as companies adopt more flexible and agile operating models. In the future, large multinational conglomerates will increasingly compete with smaller, more nimble networks of micro-mutinationals that create their own specialised value chains. Executives will need to consider how to strategically position themselves to take advantage of such business platforms.

24 November 2015

⇨ The above information is reprinted with kind permission from HSBC Bank plc. Please visit globalconnections.hsbc.com for further information.

'Generation fairtrade': UK teens want businesses to act more responsibly

UK teens care about global issues and want businesses to act more ethically.

UK teenagers are not the apathetic, self-interested generation they're often portrayed as – they care about global issues, want businesses to act more ethically, and are willing to take action to bring about change, according to a survey commissioned by the Fairtrade Foundation.

Dubbed 'Generation Fairtrade' – because they have grown up with the FAIRTRADE Mark, which turns 20 this week – more than eight in 10 of the UK teens surveyed (82%) said they think companies need to act more responsibly, but fewer than half (45%) said they trust companies to behave ethically.

Just one in ten believe governments and companies will improve conditions in the future, to the extent that the Fairtrade movement will no longer be needed. Calling on Fairtrade to "bring more brands under [its] influence", a 17-year-old from East Midlands added: "I don't think that the Government will do a very good job at improving things in general."

Ethical certification schemes have a key role to play in bridging their 'trust gap', as they provide an independent assurance that products have been sourced in an ethical or sustainable way. Almost all of the teens surveyed (97%) said that they see the FAIRTRADE Mark sometimes or often, making it the most widely recognised ethical label among UK teens – as other research has found with UK adults.

Far from being self-absorbed, 'Generation Fairtrade' care about a wide range of global issues, with more than half saying they are fairly or extremely worried about issues that Fairtrade works to address such as inequality, poverty, workers' rights, human rights, child labour and climate change. The vast majority (nine in ten) say they are willing to take action on issues they care about, with buying an ethical product being their most popular course of action.

More than three-quarters of UK teens (78%) say they would do something online to support a good cause, such as signing an online petition, liking a page on Facebook or sharing links with friends. But they will also actively participate to bring about change, with 40% saying they would take part in an event, 40% saying they would join a group or society, and 44% saying they would volunteer for a good cause.

The survey found that the market for ethical products could increase as teens begin to earn and spend their own money, as nearly two-thirds (62%) said they would like to see more Fairtrade at home and three-quarters said they wanted to buy more ethical and sustainable products – presenting an opportunity for brands who can bring ethical products to the market at a price point this generation can afford.

Young people also believe that Fairtrade will continue to play an important role in the future. More than half of those surveyed (55%) think more people will demand Fairtrade in the future and that there will be more Fairtrade products. A 20-year-old from north-east England said: "I hope that Fairtrade, and other like organisations, flourish and continue to improve conditions and equality for all."

Commenting on the survey's findings, Michael Gidney, Chief Executive of the Fairtrade Foundation, said: "From fast fashion to constant upgrades to their smartphones you might be forgiven for thinking that today's teens only care about a product's price tag and whether it looks cool enough to be Instagrammed. But 'Generation Fairtrade' also care deeply about some of the biggest global issues that we face. They have grown up with Fairtrade products at home and may even have attended one of the UK's 1,000 Fairtrade schools – so they are aware that by taking a simple action such as buying Fairtrade or signing an online petition, they can persuade businesses and governments to act more ethically – and the good news for all of us is that they want to use their power to change the world for the better."

Caroline Holme, Director at GlobeScan, who carried out the research, said: "Young people are just as switched on to global

issues as older generations and we see a similar gap in perceptions between trust and expectations of companies. The number of thoughtful answers to unprompted questions far exceeded what we typically see in online surveys. Young people are highly engaged and they want to have a say on the role of companies and organisations like Fairtrade as they step into adulthood."

20-year-old campaigner and member of Oxfam Cymru youth board, Gabriel Marques-Worssam will debate the findings of Fairtrade's research on young consumers with business leaders and representatives from government and civil society, at next week's 'Fair Future' conference in London. The event on 15 October will bring together Fairtrade producers, businesses, NGOs, campaigners, academics and politicians to explore how the Fairtrade movement can build on the achievements of the last 20 years to create a fairer future and deliver lasting change for farmers, workers, their families and communities.

Fairtrade benefits 1.4 million farmers and workers in more than 70 developing countries, by ensuring they receive a fair, stable price for their produce, better working conditions, and a Fairtrade Premium that can be invested in their business or in projects that will benefit their community, such as classrooms, clinics, clean drinking water or climate adaptation programmes.

In 2013 alone, UK shoppers bought an estimated £1.7 billion of Fairtrade products, which resulted in over £26 million of Fairtrade Premiums being paid to producers.

11 October 2014

⇨ The above information is reprinted with kind permission from the Fairtrade Foundation. Please visit www.fairtrade.org. uk for further information.

Come together, right now: countries are working with neighbours like never before

An article from The Conversation.

Nicola Yeates, Professor of Social Policy, The Open University

The European Union has never been so unpopular among its member populations; for many political parties across the continent, the whole EU project of integration and co-operation is dying, or was a mistake in the first place.

So it may come as surprise that, all over the world, deeper regional integration is favoured as a promising solution to a range of seemingly intractable social problems.

Across South America, Africa, Asia and Europe the potential development dividends of strengthening regional social regulation, social standards, social rights and redistribution have gained significant ground. From international organisations through to governments, labour and peoples' movements, regional cooperation is at the heart of major political and social reforms.

This was not always the case: regionalism's traditionally limited ambitions usually meant little more than creating hubs for markets, trade and finance. Today, regional agendas are radically reshaping and speeding up all kinds of social policy: enhancing access to affordable medicines, extending social protection, universalising health care, and promoting educational cooperation.

Keeping up

The reasons it works are obvious enough. Regional networks give countries access to a much broader menu of policy options, including tools for advancing their own social standards much faster than can be achieved through negotiations involving hundreds of countries. For smaller and developing countries in particular, regional formations can offer influence over vital global policy areas from which they could otherwise find themselves excluded.

This means more developed countries can force social standards upwards in poorer neighbour states, while smaller countries can have a strong collective blocking effect on the otherwise unfettered ambitions of larger ones.

Regional strategies are also a powerful way to resist some of the excesses of neo-liberal globalisation. Too often, global trade thrives on tax exemptions for local and global companies in ways that erode countries' domestic fiscal capacity and resources, but if regional partners can establish common trade and tax rules, they can help strengthen each other against some of the harsher effects of global capital flows.

These common rules create the 'policy space' for countries to resist downward pressures on social standards, while also helping to generate resources to fund better social provision.

And above all, good regional cooperation can often mean the difference between life and death.

Serious business

When there aren't enough health workers and health systems are weak, population health suffers and people die – a phenomenon all too relevant given the current Ebola disaster.

The reasons for these shortages are many and complex, and not all of them can be solved with cooperation. But if countries can roll their domestic initiatives together into regional strategies, pooling their resources, sharing expertise and promoting labour mobility across borders, they can start to scale up provision and address the terrible capacity issues that have left them vulnerable to major disease outbreaks and health crises.

Again, regional organisations are fast becoming the key engine in the development of other progressive social policies outside of health. For example, the Economic Community of West African States has established a regional court of justice adjudicating on national labour rights, while the Union of South American Nations (UNASUR) is now driving initiatives to expand entitlements to health care and social security; it is shaping policies around disability all over the world.

South America, of course, boasts a wide range of leftist governments keen to seize the initiative on progressive social policy – but the appetite for regional responses is felt more widely than that. International organisations are also starting to wake up to the role that empowered regional groupings can play in international economic and social development.

The EU, the Pan-American Health Organization and even the World Bank have all started to get behind new kinds of regionalism in pursuit of greater health equity.

Increasingly, then, the case is being made for regional integration as the answer to global development problems. But currently missing from these debates is a specific focus on global poverty and on the 1.2 billion people still living in extreme poverty.

A new beginning?

The debate on how to solve poverty is a crucial opportunity to think harder about the potential contributions of regionalist stances to social and economic policy.

Many regional bodies have formally declared their commitment to tackling poverty as part of their mandates and development plans, but it remains to be seen whether they are fully implementing their commitments, and how effective they are when they do. Still, they deserve their chance – and they are now getting it.

With 2015 rapidly approaching, around the world, the global poverty reduction goals set some 15 years ago are widely expected to be missed.

Given that the usual approaches to development have let these goals slip by, the potential to better harness regional collective action for pro-poor development needs to be seriously explored as a matter of urgency.

Regionalism may be facing a serious backlash within Europe, but the rest of the world has a growing appetite for it. Regional social policy will get the limelight on the 2014 UN Day for the Eradication of Poverty, whose theme is "Leave no-one behind: think, decide and act together against extreme poverty." And it needs to be far more prominent in the post-2015 development agenda.

Above all, the UN, the World Bank, and other international donors and partners, alongside governments and civil society at large, all have a vital role to play: they must enable regional groupings of nations to take robust collective action to eradicate poverty and defend human rights everywhere.

17 October 2014

⇨ The above information is reprinted with kind permission from *The Conversation*. Please visit www.theconversation.com for further information.

Has globalisation reached its high-water mark?

Those of us who still believe in free trade as the most effective route to prosperity have quite a fight on our hands.

By Jeremy Warner

Every time there is a G20 Summit, participating nations will with ritual gravity put their names to a communiqué declaring the sanctity of free trade and evils of protectionism. Then they return home and practise the opposite. Modern protectionism rarely comes in the brazen form characterised by the notorious Smoot-Hawley Tariff Act of 1930, which imposed draconian taxes on imports to the US and arguably deepened the Great Depression.

Rather it makes its appearance in subtler, backdoor forms which tend to escape World Trade Organization definitions and sanctions – subsidies to local industries, restrictions, unduly onerous standards, bans on health and safety grounds, and so on. Yet they can be no less potent in their beggar-thy-neighbour effects.

When Peugeot was bailed out by the French Government, for instance, a condition of the state aid was that the company close down its Czech production line. According to Global Trade Alert's Simon Evenett, such forms of protectionism have been growing like topsy since the onset of the financial crisis.

Despite all the optimism around American attempts to forge free trade agreements with Asia and Europe, progress is in reality depressingly slow. The global, multilateral free-trade agenda has meanwhile been mired in apparently irreconcilable differences for more than a decade.

It would nevertheless be wrong to regard these protectionist pressures as a prime cause of what is now an extraordinarily unusual slow down in global trade growth. In fact, they are much more likely to be a response to it. When export growth becomes harder to achieve, countries naturally turn in on themselves, find ways of supporting domestic demand, and if they can, disadvantaging foreign goods and services.

It's been called "peak globalisation", and it is a good term for what is now not just a fashionable theory but an observable phenomenon. June saw a little bit of an uptick in global trade, but the trend is unambiguously down. In the second quarter of this year, the volume of global trade fell 0.5%, following a fall of 1.5% in the first quarter, according to new data. This is the first such fall in global trade since the collapse of Lehman's.

It may be that June's bounce presages the beginning of an anaemic recovery, yet scarcely anyone believes that international trade is about to return to pre-crisis levels of growth. In the boom years of globalisation, cross-border trade grew twice as quickly as world output as a whole, and was widely seen as a key driver of rising living standards.

Yet, since the financial crisis, trade has consistently lagged output, and now seems to point to an outright recession. Whatever else the post-crisis $11.3 trillion of central bank money printing may have achieved, it has not succeeded in reviving the upward march in free movement of goods and services.

The positive view of this reversal is that it is more an indication of benign and in some respects quite welcome structural changes in the global economy than another cyclical catastrophe. Much of the pre-crisis boom in global trade was driven by the Asian development story, which both sucked in huge quantities of raw materials and dumped container loads of finished goods on Western markets. The internationalisation of supply chain management together with the cost efficiencies of containerisation turbo-charged the process.

China was taught a hard lesson by the post-Lehman collapse in trade.

Determination since then to shift from a less investment/export dependent form of development to one more based on domestic consumption has changed the nature of the game. The export component in Chinese output has shrunk significantly.

Many Western companies have similarly chosen to meet the challenge of growing environmental and geo-political risk by swapping offshoring for onshoring. What's more, economies will naturally become more service-based as they grow and mature, with the tradable goods sector becoming less important, something we have long been familiar with here in the UK. This may now be happening on a global scale.

The fall off in international trade is matched only by the increase in cross-border labour migration, now in nominal terms at unprecedented levels. One form of globalisation appears to be giving way to what may be an even more politically toxic version of the same thing.

In any case, the jury is at this stage out on whether the hiatus in global trade growth is the result of "peak globalisation" or the even more trendy theory among those of a Left-wing persuasion of "secular stagnation", the idea that free market capitalism has sunk into a semi-permanent state of torpor that demands extreme levels of fiscal stimulus and government intervention.

I'm with the optimists. Yet those of us who still believe in free trade as the most effective route to prosperity and to boot, the best antidote yet invented to human conflict, have quite a fight on our hands defending it from the forces of reaction.

27 August 2015

⇨ The above information is reprinted with kind permission from *The Telegraph*. Please visit www.telegraph.co.uk for further information.

What if we've reached peak globalisation?

With world trade contracting, the UK will need to promote renewables to reduce import dependency and boost regional economic growth.

By James Meadway

World trade has fallen by its largest amount since the financial crisis of 2008. The crash itself produced a significant shrinking of global trade – the sharpest since the Great Depression. At the time it was possible to believe that this was a temporary wobble. Ongoing technological change, from containerisation of freight transport to today's ubiquitous digital communications, would lock the economy into a path of deeper and deeper 'globalisation', with international flows of goods, services and money overwhelming states and transforming societies.

The rapid recovery in global trade in the first years after the crash kindled a hope that the forward march of globalisation would continue. This now looks excessively optimistic.

Over the three decades prior to the crash, global trade grew faster than the global economy. But dwarfing even this rise in trade was the extraordinary growth in cross-border financial flows, which ballooned from $500 billion (£329 billion) in 1980 to a peak of $11.8 trillion in 2007. Far outstripping the expansion of the world economy or global trade, the internationalisation of finance represented the cutting edge of globalisation – critically dependent on computing power and telecommunications.

Peak globalisation

Since 2011, however, world trade has grown significantly less rapidly than global GDP, and has now begun to shrink even as the global economy grows. World financial flows are down 60% since the pre-crash peak. International capital flows today are equivalent to 1.6% of global GDP, down from 16% of global GDP in 2007. The 'home bias' of investments has hugely increased. And capital flows into and out of the UK fell by 82% from 2007 to 2011.

Has globalisation peaked? Two fundamental factors suggest it may have. First, the financial crisis itself revealed the systemic weaknesses inherent in an over-extended financial system. Major financial institutions, banks chief among them, are now significantly more wary about reaching beyond their home bases. In the event of a future crisis, they will require strong, supportive states ready to back them up. This has drawn banks and states closer together, with weak states and weak banks propping each other up, as in the eurozone's 'sovereign-bank nexus' (the strong links between government debt and banks).

Second, states themselves are acting strategically. Globalisation was associated with a belief in the supreme merits of government inaction on the economy, but governments are increasingly strategic economic actors.

China is attempting an immense shift away from its decades-old role as low-cost exporter to the world, expanding both its domestic market, and seeking to create a new, regional trading block around the new Silk Road. The collapse of its stock market, naturally, necessitated a huge (if deeply flawed) government intervention. Protectionism is on the rise, whilst yuan devaluation has raised the spectre of 'currency wars'. The German state, meanwhile, is an assiduous defender of its own interests as a manufacturing exporter.

The UK's trade problem

The UK, too, is acting strategically. But it has been down a very

particular path. With its record-breaking current account deficit – the gap between exports and imports, plus earnings from abroad minus payments to abroad – the UK is dependent on the willingness of the rest of the world to finance its domestic expenditure.

During the high period of globalisation this was not difficult. Financial flows grew across the globe. Some of those global investors were happy to buy assets from, and make loans to, those in the UK. The UK's external debt, as a result, is amongst the highest in the world, balanced out by its ownership of assets abroad. But the presence of those flows meant that the current account did not act as a serious constraint on domestic economic activity.

Post-2008, that happy situation no longer exists. The deficit with the rest of the world still requires financing. But that makes maintaining a global financial hub, in an era of weakened financial flows, a painfully expensive necessity. Austerity is the consequence of the decision to support that hub, as George Osborne admitted in his recent House of Lords select committee hearing. By keeping

domestic government expenditure low today, the government can hope for 'fiscal space' to deal with crises tomorrow. Meanwhile, Osborne is back in China, attempting to drum up additional financial flows of investment into the UK.

This support for financial services is the strategic choice the rest of us are forced into. It means a permanent exposure to financial shocks elsewhere, a weakened domestic economy dependent on debt creation, and the steady disintegration of the welfare state through austerity.

Though they can play a part, the solution to the external deficit will not lie through exports. Devaluation of the pound since 2008 barely dented this deficit. Exports are dominated by a tiny handful of firms, with the top 5% of UK manufacturing exporters accounting for 69% of all manufacturing exports. This is a very slender base on which to build, and, even then, attempting to sell into an increasingly competitive and potentially declining global market is hardly an encouraging prospect.

Worse yet, the rising deficit itself is now being driven, in part, by the rising demands for payments that the UK's vast external debt requires.

This flow of funding is liable to stop at some point, provoking an old-fashioned sterling crisis.

Better, instead, to intervene directly in the domestic economy. Import dependency would be weakened through the promotion of domestic energy production, exploiting an obvious UK advantage in renewables. It would mean working to build effective, functioning regional economies through large-scale infrastructure investment, state-led as needed. Above all, to match changing times, the economic thinking that has dominated UK policy for three decades must also now shift.

28 September 2015

⇨ The above information is reprinted with kind permission from *The Guardian*. Please visit www.theguardian.com for further information.

Digital globalisation: the new era of global flows

Soaring flows of data and information now generate more economic value than the global goods trade.

By James Manyika, Susan Lund, Jacques Bughin, Jonathan Woetzel, Kalin Stamenov and Dhruv Dhingra

Conventional wisdom says that globalisation has stalled. But although the global goods trade has flattened and cross-border capital flows have declined sharply since 2008, globalisation is not heading into reverse. Rather, it is entering a new phase defined by soaring flows of data and information.

Remarkably, digital flows – which were practically non-existent just 15 years ago – now exert a larger impact on GDP growth than the centuries-old trade in goods, according to a new McKinsey Global Institute (MGI) report, *Digital globalization: The new era of global flows*. And although this shift makes it possible for companies to reach international markets with less capital-intensive business models, it poses new risks and policy challenges as well.

The world is more connected than ever, but the nature of its connections has changed in a fundamental way. The amount of cross-border bandwidth that is used has grown 45 times larger since 2005. It is projected to increase by an additional nine times over the next five years as flows of information, searches, communication, video, transactions and intracompany traffic continue to surge. In addition to transmitting valuable streams of information and ideas in their own right, data flows enable the movement of goods, services, finance and people. Virtually every type of cross-border transaction now has a digital component.

Trade was once largely confined to advanced economies and their large multinational companies. Today, a more digital form of globalisation has opened the door to developing countries, to small companies and start-ups, and to billions of individuals. Tens of millions of small and midsize enterprises worldwide have turned themselves into exporters by joining e-commerce marketplaces such as Alibaba, Amazon, eBay, Flipkart and Rakuten. Approximately 12 per cent of the global goods trade is conducted via international e-commerce. Even the smallest enterprises can be born global: 86 per cent of tech-based start-ups surveyed by MGI report some type of cross-border activity. Today, even the smallest firms can compete with the largest multinationals.

Individuals are using global digital platforms to learn, find work, showcase their talent, and build personal networks. Some 900 million people have international connections on social media, and 360 million take part in cross-border e-commerce. Digital platforms for both traditional employment and freelance assignments are beginning to create a more global labour market.

In this increasingly digital era of globalisation, large companies can manage their international operations in leaner, more efficient ways. Using digital platforms and tools, they can sell in fast-growing markets while keeping virtual teams connected in real time. This is a moment for companies to rethink their organisational structures, products, assets and competitors.

Global flows of all types support growth by raising productivity, and data flows are amplifying this effect by broadening participation and creating more efficient markets. MGI's analysis finds that over a decade, all types of flows acting together have raised world GDP by 10.1 per cent over what would have resulted in a world without any cross-border flows. This value amounted to some $7.8 trillion in 2014 alone, and data flows account for $2.8 trillion of this impact. Both inflows and outflows matter for growth, as they expose economies to ideas, research, technologies, talent and best practices from around the world.

Although there is substantial value at stake, not all countries are making the most of this potential. The latest MGI *Connectedness Index* – which ranks 139 countries on inflows and outflows of goods, services, finance, people, and data – finds large gaps between a handful of leading countries and the rest of the world. Singapore tops the latest rankings, followed by The Netherlands, the United States, and Germany. China has grown more connected, reaching number seven, but advanced economies in general remain more connected than developing countries. In fact, each type of flow is concentrated among a small set of highly connected countries.

Lagging countries are closing the gaps with the leaders at a very slow pace, and their limited participation has had a real cost to the world economy. If the rest of the world had increased its participation in global flows at the same rate as the top quartile over the past decade, world GDP would be $10 trillion, or 13 percent, higher today. For countries that have been slow to participate, the opportunities for catch-up growth are too substantial to ignore.

February 2016

⇨ The above information is reprinted with kind permission from McKinsey & Company. Please visit www.mckinsey.com for further information.

Australia seeking free trade deal with UK following Brexit vote

Prime Minister Theresa May calls her counterpart to discuss deal as Liam Fox claims "around a dozen" other deals are being looked at ready for when Britain leaves the EU.

By Arj Singh

Australia has called for a free trade deal with Britain as soon as possible, in a Brexit boost for Prime Minister Theresa May.

Ms May spoke to her Australian counterpart Malcolm Turnbull on Saturday, who expressed his desire to open up trading between the two Commonwealth countries as a matter of urgency.

The new PM described the call as "very encouraging" and insisted it showed leaving the European Union could work for Britain.

She tasked newly appointed International Trade Secretary Liam Fox to begin exploring options and he has told the *Sunday Times* that he is "scoping" around 12 other deals.

Ms May said: "I have been very clear that this Government will make a success of our exit from the European Union.

"One of the ways we will do this is by embracing the opportunities to strike free trade deals with our partners across the globe.

"It is very encouraging that one of our closest international partners is already seeking to establish just such a deal.

"This shows that we can make Brexit work for Britain, and the new Secretary of State for International Trade will be taking this forward in the weeks and months ahead.

"Britain is an outward-looking and globally-minded country, and we will build on this as we forge a new role for ourselves in the world."

On Friday, Ms May told Scottish First Minister Nicola Sturgeon she would not trigger Article 50 to leave the EU before getting UK-wide agreement, a potentially difficult objective given Scotland voted overwhelmingly to remain in the bloc.

But Dr Fox claimed numerous non-EU countries had already asked Britain for a trade deal and said he was "scoping about a dozen free trade deals outside the EU to be ready for when we leave" – potentially in January 2019 – amid reports that he was preparing to fly to the United States next week.

He told the *Sunday Times*: "We've already had a number of countries saying, 'We'd love to do a trade deal with the world's fifth biggest economy without having to deal with the other 27 members of the EU.'"

17 July 2016

⇨ The above information is reprinted with kind permission from the Press Association. Please visit www.pressassociation.com for further information.

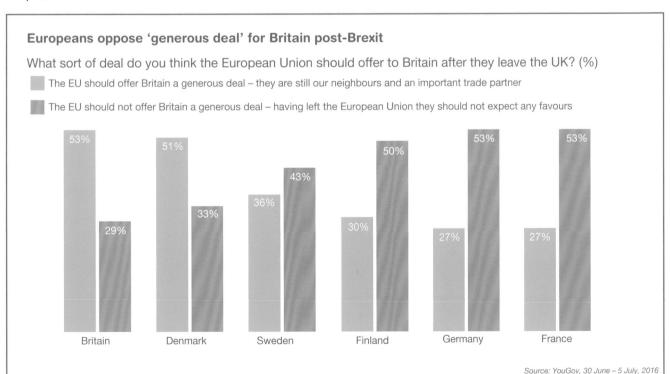

Europeans oppose 'generous deal' for Britain post-Brexit

What sort of deal do you think the European Union should offer to Britain after they leave the UK? (%)

The EU should offer Britain a generous deal – they are still our neighbours and an important trade partner

The EU should not offer Britain a generous deal – having left the European Union they should not expect any favours

	Britain	Denmark	Sweden	Finland	Germany	France
Generous	53%	51%	36%	30%	27%	27%
Not generous	29%	33%	43%	50%	53%	53%

Source: YouGov, 30 June – 5 July, 2016

Post Brexit vote, a fresh look at globalisation

The UK is withdrawing from one of the greatest projects of economic integration, argues David Lipton.

There were a lot of dramatic headlines over the weekend suggesting that Brexit signals the beginning of the end of globalisation. Surely, it is too soon to understand all the ramifications of the British referendum. But at the same time, today is surely a good day to make the case for multilateralism. While there are plenty of reasons to be concerned about the future, I will argue that globalisation still has promise. But to achieve that promise, we will need a fresh look at multilateralism and the role the international financial institutions can play.

My generation can be excused for assuming that history moves in one direction: we have experienced globalisation and with it rising incomes and economic progress at home and abroad. Our experience was different than our parents' generation, which came of age experiencing depression and war.

But now the Brexit vote raises the possibility of an abrupt change in direction. While that vote may have hinged on sentiments about migration and sovereignty, its effect will be the withdrawal of the UK from one of the greatest projects of economic integration.

European unity has been part of our generation's narrative. From the creation of the coal and steel community in 1951, to the creation of the euro, to the re-integration of central and eastern Europe. Brexit is, at the least, an interruption in that integration process.

Could the same doubts that gave rise to Brexit lead to an interruption in globalisation?

Many people say globalisation is unstoppable. Integration has been achieved. There is no going back. I hope so. But Brexit and the economic trends in the world should cause us to pause, and to think again about irreversibility.

Despite decades of deepening integration, many have come to question whether closer global integration will bring them meaningful benefits, and they see costs and vulnerabilities, both economic, but also social and cultural. Without clear economic benefits, the costs, including a sense of lack of control, can dominate public opinion.

The critics can point to evidence: for people in advanced economies, the global financial crisis was a hit to wealth and, for many, retirement prospects; and growth recovery is still sluggish. People feel the effects of income inequality, stagnating wages, and a lack of job security; and they sense and fear market volatility.

At one level, we have to admit that there are some economic forces at play we don't yet fully understand: we cannot satisfactorily answer some important questions. Are we in secular stagnation? Does the trend toward lower real interest rates over the last 15 years reflect a drying up of investment possibilities? We will need to continue looking at these questions.

So what can we say? Let me make three points:

First, globalisation has lifted hundreds of millions of people out of poverty and raised the living standards across the globe. There is every reason to believe it still holds the promise of supporting rising living standards in advanced economies and emerging markets and developing countries alike. But to preserve and protect that promise, we will have to work to enhance the gains of globalisation, limit the costs and vulnerabilities, and make the case to a skeptical public.

Second, as has always been the case, much of what needs to be done requires action at the individual country level. We at the Fund have called for a three-pronged approach to boosting growth, with support for demand coming from both fiscal and monetary policies, and with structural reforms tailored to support demand in the short run

and to boost potential growth over time. While this remains the right recipe, it is clear that individual governments see limits to their room for manoeuvre, and so far have not made sufficient progress.

And third, we need multilateralism now more than ever. Part of the political problem today is that national leaders cannot really solve domestic problems, nor fulfil the aspirations of their people, with domestic action. That is because their country's prospects depend too heavily on global prospects.

So, we need everyone pushing in the same direction at the same time. That is why it is important for the IMF to rally its membership to act in harmony. With each country doing its part, the impact will be greater, and leaders can have some greater assurance that growth will be based on demand creation, not demand diversion.

And we also need to consider how to make sure that the international monetary system is supportive of individual country efforts, creating growth opportunities and lowering vulnerabilities.

When I say this, I have a couple things in mind. Even if the advanced economies are facing a form of secular stagnation, in principle the emerging markets and developing countries hold the potential to be the engine of growth over the next generation, as rapid growth leads to convergence in living standards toward advanced levels. However, we are seeing a perverse slowdown in potential growth in emerging markets and developing countries. With present projections, many large emerging markets cannot expect to see convergence at all. That is perverse because with the availability of technology, Internet communications creating educational opportunities, and ample funds for investment, those countries should be accelerating and speeding convergence in living standards.

Now surely, emerging markets and developing countries still have much to do at home to adjust to global events and foster faster growth. But the volatility of the global economy and especially of large flows of short-term capital has not been helping. Rather it is leading emerging markets and developing countries to have to act defensively, guarding against openness, worrying about borrowing and current account deficits, and self-insuring with weak currencies and reserve accumulation.

Re-examination of the international monetary system can help here. We can re-assess how macro prudential and capital flow measures can provide protection. We can ask how to promote growth supporting equity flows. And how we can better promote technology transfer.

And we can create a better global financial safety net, including through IMF coordination with regional financing arrangements, and possibly new IMF lending facilities.

There is also room for cooperation with the new multilateral institutions like the Asian Infrastructure Investment Bank, whose formation we welcome.

Let me end by observing that the new normal in global economics has a parallel in global politics. Ian Bremmer of the Eurasia Group has dubbed this a "G-zero", a world characterised by a "vacuum of global governance". Hegemony, for better or worse, no longer prevails. Nor are traditional security relationships coping with the evolution of security challenges. With a growing number of important geo-political risks, and their adverse impacts on economic growth and stability, we will need to pay more attention to the interplay between economics and geopolitics. We see this already in addressing events in the Middle East, Africa, and the refugee issue in Europe.

In the economic realm, the IMF can be a voice for global cooperation and collective action. The IMF is stronger than ever, and better able to deal with economic challenges. Now we must continue to address the new challenges that arise with creative, multilateral solutions that can respond to our rapidly changing world.

30 June 2016

⇨ The above information is reprinted with kind permission from the International Monetary Fund. Please visit www.imf.org for further information.

Brexit is a rejection of globalisation

The EU has failed to protect its population from a global economic model that many believe is not working for them.

By Larry Elliott

The age of globalisation began on the day the Berlin Wall came down. From that moment in 1989, the trends evident in the late 1970s and throughout the 1980s accelerated: the free movement of capital, people and goods; trickle-down economics; a much diminished role for nation states; and a belief that market forces, now unleashed, were unstoppable.

There has been push back against globalisation over the years. The violent protests seen in Seattle during the World Trade Organization meeting in December 1999 were the first sign that not everyone saw the move towards untrammelled freedom in a positive light. One conclusion from the 9/11 attacks on New York and Washington in September 2001 was that it was not only trade and financial markets that had gone global. The collapse of the investment bank Lehman Brothers seven years later put paid to the idea that the best thing governments could do when confronted with the power of global capital was to get out of the way and let the banks supervise themselves.

Now we have Britain's rejection of the EU. This was more than a protest against the career opportunities that never knock and the affordable homes that never get built. It was a protest against the economic model that has been in place for the past three decades.

To be sure, not all Britain's problems are the result of its EU membership. It is not the European Commission's fault that productivity is so weak or that the trains don't run on time. The deep-seated failings that were there when Britain voted in the referendum last Thursday were still there when the country woke up to the result on Friday.

Evidence of just how unbalanced the economy is will be provided when the latest figures for Britain's current account are released later this week. These show whether the country's trade and investment income are in the black or the red. At the last count, in the final three months of 2015, the UK was running a record peacetime deficit of 7% of GDP.

In another sense, however, the EU is culpable. In the shiny new world created when former communist countries were integrated into the global model, Europe was supposed to be big and powerful enough to protect its citizens against the worst excesses of the market. Nation states had previously been the guarantor of full employment and welfare. The controls they imposed on the free movement of capital and people ensured that trade unions could bargain for higher pay without the threat of work being off-shored, or cheaper labour being brought into the country.

In the age of globalisation, the idea was that a more integrated Europe would collectively serve as the bulwark that nation states could no longer provide. Britain, France, Germany or Italy could not individually resist the power of transnational capital, but the EU potentially could. The way forward was clear. Move on from a single market to a single currency, a single banking system, a single budget and eventually a single political entity.

That dream is now over. As Charles Grant, the director of the Centre for European Reform thinktank put it: "Brexit is a momentous event in the history of Europe and from now on the narrative will be one of disintegration not integration."

The reason is obvious. Europe has failed to fulfil the historic role allocated to it. Jobs, living standards and welfare states were all better protected in the heyday of nation states in the 1950s and 1960s than they have been in the age of globalisation.

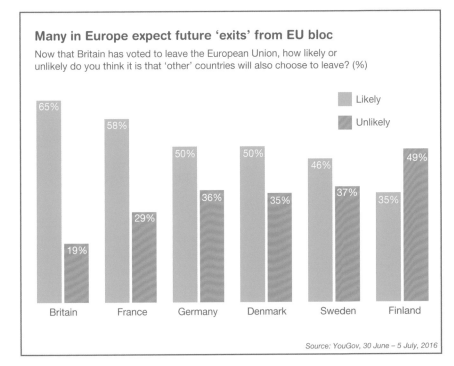

Many in Europe expect future 'exits' from EU bloc

Now that Britain has voted to leave the European Union, how likely or unlikely do you think it is that 'other' countries will also choose to leave? (%)

Likely / Unlikely

Britain 65% / 19%
France 58% / 29%
Germany 50% / 36%
Denmark 50% / 35%
Sweden 46% / 37%
Finland 35% / 49%

Source: YouGov, 30 June – 5 July, 2016

Unemployment across the eurozone is more than 10%. Italy's economy is barely any bigger now than it was when the euro was created. Greece's economy has shrunk by almost a third. Austerity has eroded welfare provision. Labour market protections have been stripped away.

Inevitably, there has been a backlash, manifested in the rise of populist parties on the left and right. An increasing number of voters believe there is not much on offer from the current system. They think globalisation has benefited a small privileged elite, but not them. They think it is unfair that they should pay the price for bankers' failings. They hanker after a return to the security that the nation state provided, even if that means curbs on the core freedoms that underpin globalisation, including the free movement of people.

This has caused great difficulties for Europe's mainstream parties, but especially those of the centre left. They have been perfectly happy to countenance the idea of curbs on capital movements such as a financial transaction tax, and have no problems with imposing tariffs to prevent the dumping of Chinese steel. They feel uncomfortable, however, with the idea that there should be limits on the free movement of people.

The risk is that if the mainstream parties don't respond to the demands of their traditional supporters, they will be replaced by populist parties who will. The French Socialist Party has effectively lost most of its old blue-collar working class base to the hard left and the hard right, and in the UK there is a danger that the same thing will happen to the Labour Party, where Jeremy Corbyn's laissez-faire approach to immigration is at odds with the views of many voters in the north that supported Ed Miliband in the 2015 general election, but who plumped for Brexit last week.

There are those who argue that globalisation is now like the weather, something we can moan about but not alter. This is a false comparison. The global market economy was created by a set of political decisions in the past and it can be shaped by political decisions taken in the future.

Torsten Bell, the director of the Resolution Foundation thinktank, analysed the voting patterns in the referendum and found that those parts of Britain with the strongest support for Brexit were those that had been poor for a long time. The result was affected by "deeply entrenched national geographical inequality", he said.

There has been much lazy thinking in the past quarter of a century about globalisation. As Bell notes, it is time to rethink the assumption that a "flexible globalised economy can generate prosperity that is widely shared".

Self-evidently, large numbers of people across Europe do not believe a flexible, globalised economy is working for them. One response to the Brexit vote from the rest of Europe has been that a tough line should be taken with Britain to show other countries that dissent has consequences. This would only make matters worse. Voters have legitimate grievances about an economic system that has failed them. Punishing Britain will not safeguard the EU. It will hasten its dissolution.

26 June 2016

⇨ The above information is reprinted with kind permission from *The Guardian*. Please visit www.theguardian.com for further information.

Key facts

⇨ Globalisation refers to the process by which the world's local and regional economies, societies, and cultures have become integrated together through a global network of communication, transportation and trade. (page 5)

⇨ New research from Mintel's flagship British Lifestyles report finds that three quarters (74%) of UK consumers claim to have felt at least one benefit of globalisation personally, with over half (53%) feeling three or more benefits. (page 7)

⇨ 62% of Younger Millennials and 63% of Older Millennials claiming to have felt three or more benefits of globalisation. (page 7)

⇨ Over half (55%) of Brits agree that access to cheaper technology products benefits Britain as a country and 51% say it benefits them personally. Furthermore, cheaper international travel is seen as a benefit to Britain by 50% of UK consumers, whilst 44% agree it benefits them personally. (page 7)

⇨ Four in five (79%) claim that Britain doing business and trading with other countries benefits Britain as a country, whilst 78% say the same of global companies investing in Britain. Additionally, two thirds (66%) say that job opportunities at international companies in Britain benefits the UK, whilst 64% say the same of cultural links between Britain and other countries. (page 8)

⇨ Together the US and EU account for around €22 trillion in annual trade, almost half of the world total. (page 10)

⇨ The US imposed financial sanctions on North Korea in 2005, adding to an aid and trade embargo that had been in place for some time. It turned out that the financial sanctions were a major blow to the North Korean Government; far more effective than the regime that had been in place, and more effective than expected by the US administration. (page 14)

⇨ New figures today (18 April 2016) show a record number of UK businesses interested in exporting through government-brokered opportunities, with over 20,000 responses since November 2015. (page 15)

⇨ Over the last five years, UK aid has reached millions across the world. It has supported 11 million children through school. It has distributed 47 million bed nets, contributing to malaria deaths falling by 60% over the last 15 years. And it has supported over 60 million people to access clean water, better sanitation or improved hygiene conditions. (page 22)

⇨ New research from the McKinsey Global Institute looked at how all types of global flows influence economic growth. It found that over the course of a decade, cross-border flows of goods, services, finance, people, and data increased world GDP by roughly ten per cent over what would have occurred in a world without any flows. This value was equivalent to $7.8 trillion in 2014 alone. (page 24)

⇨ Dubbed 'Generation Fairtrade' – because they have grown up with the FAIRTRADE Mark – more than eight in ten of the UK teens surveyed (82%) said they think companies need to act more responsibly, but fewer than half (45%) said they trust companies to behave ethically. (page 28)

⇨ More than half of those surveyed (55%) think more people will demand Fairtrade in the future and that there will be more Fairtrade products. (page 28)

⇨ In 2013 alone, UK shoppers bought an estimated £1.7 billion of Fairtrade products, which resulted in over £26 million of Fairtrade Premiums being paid to producers. (page 29)

⇨ In the second quarter of this year, the volume of global trade fell 0.5%, following a fall of 1.5% in the first quarter, according to new data. This is the first such fall in global trade since the collapse of Lehman's. (page 31)

⇨ Since 2011, world trade has grown significantly less rapidly than global GDP, and has now begun to shrink even as the global economy grows. World financial flows are down 60% since the pre-crash peak. (page 32)

⇨ 86 per cent of tech-based start-ups surveyed by MGI report some type of cross-border activity. (page 34)

⇨ 53% of people in Britain think that the EU should offer Britain a generous deal post-Brexit. This is compared to just 27% of people in Germany and France, and 36% of people in Sweden. (page 38)

⇨ 65% of people in Britain think that more countries will decide to leave the EU now that Britain has voted to leave. (page 38)

Brexit

An abbreviation that stands for 'British exit'. Referring to the referendum that took place on 23 June 2016 where British citizens voted to exit the European Union.

Fair trade

A movement which advocates fair prices, improved working conditions and better trade terms for producers in developing countries. Exports from developing countries that have been certified Fairtrade – which include products such as coffee, tea, honey, cocoa, chocolate, sugar, cotton and bananas – carry the Fairtrade mark.

Free trade

An economic policy which promotes the free movement of goods and services between countries and the elimination of restrictions to trading between nations, such as import and export tariffs.

Gross Domestic Product (GDP)

The value of all the goods and services produced in a country within a year.

Globalisation

Globalisation is a term used to explain the increased social and trade-related exchanges between nations. It implies that nations are moving closer together economically and culturally. In recent years, through the Internet, air travel, trade and popular culture, globalisation has rapidly increased.

International Monetary Fund (IMF)

The International Monetary Fund (IMF) is an international organisation set up to oversee the global financial system and stabilise exchange rates.

Liberalisation

The relaxation of government restrictions such as barriers to free trade.

Multinational corporations (MNCs)

Powerful companies which operate in more than one country. Due to their size and large economies, multinational corporations – sometimes called transnational corporations (TNCs) – can hold substantial influence over governments and local economies.

Tariffs

A tax placed on imported and exported goods.

Trade

When you buy a computer game or a bar of chocolate, you are 'trading': exchanging money for goods. Workers, companies, countries and consumers take part in trade. Workers make or grow the goods. Companies pay the workers and sell what they produce. Governments encourage companies to set up; they create jobs, generate taxes and earn foreign currency. Consumers buy the end product.

TTIP

The Transatlantic Trade and Investment Partnership is a trade deal being negotiated between the EU and the USA.

World Bank

An organisation set up to reduce poverty by providing loans for developing countries.

World Trade Organization (WTO)

An international organisation first set up in 1995 to monitor the rules of international trade and promote free trade between countries. The WTO has the power to impose fines or sanctions on member countries that do not follow the rules of trade. Critics of the WTO argue that it holds too much power and protects the interests of rich countries to the disadvantage of developing countries.

Assignments

Brainstorming

⇨ In small groups, discuss what you know about globalisation:

  • What is globalisation?

  • What are some of the benefits of globalisation?

  • What are some of the downsides of globalisation?

Research

⇨ Research a global brand such as Panasonic and investigate how many countries they sell their products in and where they have offices/factories. Share your findings with a classmate.

⇨ Conduct a survey among your year group, your family and your friends to find out about peoples' opinions of globalisation. You should ask at least five questions to help you discover how much people know about globalisation and whether they think it is a good thing or a bad thing. Create some graphs based on your findings and share with your class.

⇨ Research either the UK's biggest imports, or its biggest exports. Make a list and compare with a partner.

⇨ Choose a point of interest from the *Globalisation Timeline* on pages 3 and 4. Research this event/ invention and create a PowerPoint presentation that explores its impact on globalisation.

⇨ Design and conduct a survey among people in your year group to find out how many of them live in a household which purchases fair trade goods. Present your findings as a set of graphs.

Design

⇨ Design a poster that explains in simple terms, and perhaps using icons or cartoons, the concept of globalisation.

⇨ Choose one of the articles from this book and create an illustration that highlights the key themes of the piece.

⇨ Imagine that you work for a fair trade organisation that is launching a new chocolate bar. Think of a name and a logo for your chocolate that will reinforce the benefits of fair trade, then design some social media images and website banners that will help you spread the word about your new product.

⇨ Use the table on page 19 to create a colour coded world map that shows the major exporters of personal, cultural and recreational services in 2013 and 2014.

Oral

⇨ As a class, debate whether globalisation is a good thing or a bad thing.

⇨ Create a PowerPoint presentation that explains the role of the World Trade Organization.

⇨ In pairs, go through this book and discuss the cartoons you come across. Think about what the artists were trying to portray with each illustration.

⇨ The article on page 28 suggests that 'UK teens want business to act more responsibly'. Do you think this is true? In small groups, discuss how important corporate responsibility is when choosing brands/products. Make a bullet point list of your key points, then compare with the other groups in your class.

⇨ Is globalisation a threat to identity? Discuss your views in small groups.

Reading/writing

⇨ Read the article *Has globalisation reached its high-water mark?* (page 31) and write a summary for your school newspaper.

⇨ How has the rise of communications technology such as the Internet and mobile phones affected globalisation? Plan and write an article examining this phenomenon.

⇨ Write a diary entry covering a day in the life of a developing-world farmer struggling to compete with the large multinationals also operating in his region.

⇨ "Brexit is a rejection of globalisation." Write an essay exploring this statement.

⇨ Write a dictionary definition of globalisation.

⇨ Write a lesson plan explaining the concept of trade sanctions. Give some real-life examples to help illustrate your lesson.

⇨ Watch the film *The Cup* (1999), in which a young boy is determined to bring a television to his Tibetan monastery in time for the World Cup, and write a review exploring the theme of globalisation throughout the story.

Acknowledgements

The publisher is grateful for permission to reproduce the material in this book. While every care has been taken to trace and acknowledge copyright, the publisher tenders its apology for any accidental infringement or where copyright has proved untraceable. The publisher would be pleased to come to a suitable arrangement in any such case with the rightful owner.

Images

All images courtesy of iStock, except pages 26, 27, 33, 37 & 39: Pixabay.

Icons

Page 1 – Cloud: Madebyoliver; Money: Roundicons; Handshake: Roundicons; Cheque: Madebyoliver; Conversation: Roundicons; Insurance: Freepik; Bus: Freepik; Backpack: Freepik; Masks: Freepik; Builder: Freepik.

Page 7 – box top right: Housing: Freepik; Food: Roundicons; Bus: Popcorn Arts.

Page 7 – box bottom left: Beer: Madebyoliver; Piggybank: Madebyoliver; Tree: Madebyoliver; Computer: Popcorn Arts.

Page 8 – Coffee: Freepik; Coke: Freepik; Holiday: Madebyoliver; Newspaper: Madebyoliver; Questionmark: Freepik; TV: Madebyoliver; Lipstick: Freepik.

Illustrations

Don Hatcher: pages 4 & 36. Simon Kneebone: pages 9 & 22. Angelo Madrid: pages 15 & 24.

Additional acknowledgements

Editorial on behalf of Independence Educational Publishers by Cara Acred.

With thanks to the Independence team: Mary Chapman, Sandra Dennis, Christina Hughes, Jackie Staines and Jan Sunderland.

Cara Acred

Cambridge

September 2016